MAKE YOUR SUNDAY SCHOOL GROW THROUGH EVALUATION

Harold J. Westing

VICTOR BOOKS

 a division of SP Publications, Inc., Wheaton, Illinois
Offices also in Fullerton, California • Whitby, Ontario, Canada • London, England

Second printing, 1977

Bible quotations are from the *New American Standard Bible* (NASB), © 1960, 1962, 1963, 1968, 1971, 1972, 1973. The Lockman Foundation, La Habra, California. Other quotations are from *The Living Bible* (LB), © 1971 Tyndale House Publishers, Wheaton, Illinois. All quotations used by permission.

Library of Congress Catalog Card Number: 76-9216
ISBN: 0-88207-464-4

VICTOR BOOKS
A division of SP Publications, Inc.
P.O. Box 1825 • Wheaton, Ill. 60187

To my wife who so patiently kept the home fires burning during so many years of travel, to Dr. Eugene Vanarski and Dr. James Carpenter for their professional advice, and to Dr. Russell Shive for his encouragement in developing and using the ministry of evaluation.

Contents

1
Going, Growing, or Glowing

"Just look at this stack of visitor cards filled out during this last year," a member of the pastoral staff said to me during a visit to his church.

"That's outstanding," I remarked. "Tell me, how many of them have become regular members?"

The answer was glum; most of the visitors had chosen not to come back. The pastor and I agreed this was a tragedy. No doubt the visitors had needs which they sensed would not be met at that church. Churches that meet people's needs fill their facilities. People drive or walk great distances, passing many churches en route, to attend a church where their lives will be enriched.

My friend's church was being evaluated every Sunday by the scrutinizing eyes of visitors. The evaluation produces a vote either to become a regular attender or to go elsewhere.

Regular members also cast their votes on the basis of steady evaluation—by attendance, involvement, and financial contribution. Once in a while the pastor gets a sample reading on people's feelings through some casual comment or probing question, but most of the data which could guide church ministries goes unrecorded.

It is easy and persuasive to say that we are accountable to the Lord, not to visitors or even the congregation, for the nature of our church program. Why should we measure our ministry by what every Tom, Dick, and Mary say about it?

Some pastors quote Isaiah 55:11 and declare that God's Word will produce fruit as long as we are giving it out. "So shall My Word be which goeth forth out of My mouth: it shall not return unto Me empty without accomplishing what I desire, and with succeeding in the matter for which I sent it." It is true that God's implanted Word generates life in receptive hearts, but we can do many things to encourage openness to His seed—truth. If this were not so, we would do nothing but read Scripture in church services, and on street corners, then depart till the next meeting.

What if a devout farmer said, "God, I've dumped Your created seed on Your soil—now with your sun and rain You make it grow"? I haven't seen any farm flourish under these circumstances.

When bugs begin to eat the foliage in my garden, I take a sample to the local green thumb expert, who thoroughly evaluates it and tells me just what spray to use. Years of research enable the expert to prescribe the right action.

Some hobbyists are satisfied to raise a few flowers, while real farmers are not satisfied until they have gotten the greatest yield per acre. In the same way, some Christians are satisfied simply to be involved in God's greatest task without discerning if they are making the greatest possible impact.

God expects faithfulness, we say, suggesting that God asks us only to do our best and to leave the results with Him. But if we do not check on results, how can we know if we are genuinely giving our best? "God only requires faithfulness" may be a cover-up, I'm afraid, for laziness or for unwillingness to face the need for something more than good intentions.

Do you want to know if God's Word is being taught to more

people in your Sunday School this year than last? Or are you concerned that students are living God's Word more vitally because of your school? Are you smugly chalking up so many home visits, or are you checking on the effectiveness of these visits? Are you happy to have enlisted 10 more on the attendance rolls than last year—without knowing why you lost 30 or more?

As I interviewed a young man for a summer ministry, I asked what steps he would take in showing a student the way to Christ. In a confused response he finally admitted that he couldn't do so. Later, when I told his youth pastor why I would not be able to use him for the job, the pastor was flabbergasted. "Just recently we have gone over that time and again," he said.

On further investigation I found that the boy had been told a number of times how to lead a student to Christ, but he had not been asked to express it back to his teacher. The teacher had overlooked the fact that truth is not yours unless you are able to verbalize it to someone else. In a real-life situation—my interview—the leader's teaching was evaluated and found wanting. Having seen his weakness, however, he could approach both that boy and his next session with a sense of efficiency.

Dr. Richard Glasser, whose research led him to write *Reality Therapy* and *Schools Without Failure*, points out in the latter book a major cause for schools failing to provide a quality education: they do not help children consistently experience a sense of success. No doubt there is a significant parallel in the church. When Sunday School students begin to see the effects of Scripture in their everyday lives, they will sense a success which will stimulate them to return for more learning.

I've found only a few Sunday School staffs that have shown serious concern about the effectiveness of their teaching on student spiritual development. Yet most measure the volume of attendance and the improvements of their facilities. Progress in these areas does encourage the staff for a time, but do these results satisfy God? Are these the objectives of our ministry? Is it possible to determine whether our teaching is changing students' lives? The answers depend on your reply to another question:

Do you dare make an honest evaluation of the effectiveness of your ministry?

The writer of Proverbs tersely sums up the need for an honest look at ourselves and our ministry. "It is a badge of honor to accept valid criticism. Any enterprise is built by wise planning, becomes strong through common sense, and profits wonderfully by keeping abreast of the facts. To learn, you must want to be taught. To refuse reproof is stupid" (Prov. 25:12; 24:3-4; 12:1, LB).

Two buildings which were built in the early 1900s stood side by side, one almost as strong as the day it was built, the other about to collapse. One caretaker had crawled often under his house, examined the foundation, replaced or improved weakened timbers. The other owner didn't bother because from the outside the house looked strong. Churches and their programs, too, are often evaluated by their appearance rather than by their inner strength.

A certain church with a strong witness for many years was showing signs of decline and ineptness. The leaders accepted the fact that the law of degeneration attacked physical life and constantly threatened secular agencies and organizations, but it was hard for them to realize that Sunday Schools could also be victims of that law.

When the leaders were brave enough to look at their work honestly and thoroughly, they recognized the danger signals. Teacher standards were very low and the officers operated in a slipshod fashion. Spiritual concern was superficial. Once the leaders faced their weaknesses, they began to develop a strategy for rebuilding. By prayerful effort they regained their vitality and influenced people for Christ. They profited by honestly looking at themselves. So may you.

2
Getting There Together

"But I can't ask my Sunday School staff to be evaluated—they're all volunteers who are limited in time and motivation. We ought to be grateful for what they're doing and pray that they won't quit."

That's the fear of many Christian education leaders. But the focus is distorted. Is a salary and pressure from "the boss" the greatest incentive to do a good job? No; it may be the most prevalent spur to good work because of our materialistic society. But there is a far stronger inducement for good performance than a paycheck. And Christian service provides that incentive.

Christian workers begin their tasks with a sense of mission for God. If they are unwilling to serve sacrificially and improve their ministry through correction and growth, they have not caught an adequate vision of the glory of God and the spiritual rewards of serving Him.

Such a vision comes through effective preaching of the Word of God—and through the loving help of fellow-Christians. The Lord designed the living church to be a beautiful and productive organism—a body of varied members who not only teach each other about God, but also assist each other to grow in spiritual stature. "Let us consider how to stimulate one another to love and good deeds, not forsaking our own assembling together as is the habit of some, but encouraging one another; and all the more, as you see the day drawing near" (Heb. 10:24-25).

This passage is often cited as a reprimand to those who neglect church attendance, but this was not the main purpose of the admonition. "To stimulate one another to love and good deeds" is what should be occurring in the New Testament church—the building and the people.

And see how closely it is associated with the evaluation process. Our Lord designed the church so we would make opportunities to interact with one another and to stimulate each other toward spiritual maturity. In the current emphasis on the sharing part of Christian "body life," we should not forget body accountability.

David Augsburger said it beautifully in his book, *Caring Enough to Confront:* "When we have genuine love in the church for one another, it will be reflected not only in sharing our good things with one another but also in confronting one another with matters that need discipline and correction."

Have you ever seen yourself as a tonic? That's what this verse says each Christian ought to be. You ought to rouse others to nobler action. You are to be a stimulus so that others will produce love and good works. Somehow your relationship with other people in the body of Christ ought to help them express Christian love to others and to increase their fruitfulness in serving God. Where could this kind of encouraging be done better than among fellow workers in the Sunday School?

I questioned a new Christian about his rapid growth in the Lord. He gave the credit to a friend who had discipled him. He underlined his experience by saying, "Without some form of discipline there is no possibility of learning." Such discipline comes either from within or from another. In some cases it must come from others.

I have never seen a church family grow without discipline. It occurs when the saints discipline themselves in the ways of Christ or the members lovingly give and receive discipline.

When I participate in an evaluation and consultation in a church, I first ask the people to establish their profile of an "ideal" teacher and Sunday School. Then I ask them to indicate their actual practice and accomplishments as teachers. In almost every case there is a large gap between what they feel they ought to do and what they are actually doing. For example, they tell me they ought to be involved with their students outside of the class at least once a month, but very few of them are.

I've watched some teachers work under the supervision of different superintendents over a period of years. Their level of performance, to a great extent, depends on the kind of discipline their leaders provide. Strong Christian leaders provide the discipline that provokes their fellow workers to fruitful love and good works.

There are many natural reasons for resisting a new level of supervision and even loving direction from a group. The following suggestions will help develop a "good-deeds-provoking" team.

1. The passage from Hebrews indicates that we must give consideration to one another before we can stir one another to love and good works. This means we need to be sensitive to others and know their hurts and at what point they're stimulated. To share most deeply, we will be guided by knowledge of their backgrounds, their personalities, and their aspirations. It is helpful to be acquainted with their self-image, and how many years they have known the Lord.

When we show consideration to others, we do not talk

down to them or ignore the positive aspects of their ministry. We express sincere appreciation, perhaps as: "You are doing a fine job in the area of ————, but I have a suggestion for your consideration in the matter of ————." Remember we are serving the Lord together.

2. An evaluator does not have to be an expert, but he must earn the right to be an evaluator. This is done by working at the same level of efficiency you desire for others. As a leader you frequently ask the team, "How can we do our task better?" and you are open to their suggestions for you.

A pastor friend of mine has a meeting with his board once a year at which time his ministry is evaluated. This opens up his people to his leadership and his evaluation of their work. The whole ministry of the group must build on the assumption that we all need to grow and improve. This minimizes critical attitudes and builds strong body life.

3. An evaluation should not be attempted unless there is a definite description of responsiblities and goals, and, of course, this requires a written definition. Training must also be available to stimulate the level of expectation after an evaluation is given. Evaluation without an opportunity to improve will discourage and frustrate the worker.

4. The process of evaluation may occur without being scheduled, but it is more likely to be overlooked if there is no design or structure for the process. In a Sunday School where the "LEROY" certification program is followed, each teacher is asked to be evaluated at least once during the year in order to be a certified teacher. Under the LEROY program, teachers can improve themselves at five different levels:

L eadership Training Course taken once a year
E valuated once a year by a competent worker
    (see Observation-Evaluation Sheet and Evaluation of the Teaching-Learning Process, Appendix, pages 81-85.)

R eading at least 200 pages at his level of experience and understanding

O bserving another competent teacher at their same level

Y early conference attendance

Another beautifully designed program to facilitate the evaluation process is to ask each teacher and worker to develop a self-guided contract for a designated period of time. These could be written for a quarter or for the entire school year. The self-guided contract is in a sense a fullfillment of the Hebrews 10:24-25 passage. It asks the teacher or worker to write down the kinds of improvement which he hopes to engage in during the coming period. As he writes the contract he will agree to meet with the department superintendent or someone else on his team as the quarter or year is completed to discuss the progress made in fulfilling his goals. This body life stimulus moves teachers to great strides of growth.

SUNDAY SCHOOL WORKER'S SELF-GUIDED CONTRACT

WORKER'S NAME _____ POSITION _____
OBJECTIVES to be prayerfully accomplished during the period of time _____ to _____ .
At the end of the period I'll be discussing my progress with: _____ .
COMPLETED
1. (sample) I will plan to personally discuss with each of my 10 students his need for committing his life to Christ.
2.
3.

If a teacher does not have a good picture of what a competent teacher is, he may not understand what items to include in the schedule of events to be improved. You may choose to provide Self-Study Guides like the ones in the Appendix beginning on page 63. Of course, studying books and taking teacher training classes should provide the same kind of input.

5. Concentrate on a team concept among your staff. If all of the workers, including the teachers and the department

superintendent, feel as if they are in this ministry together, the evaluation process will be greatly facilitated. Too often teachers feel as if the classtime is theirs and the department superintendent feels as if the assembly hour is his. There must be team planning toward the total-hour teaching concept where each person has a voice in what goes on during the Sunday School hour. One of the basic concepts of team teaching is that all of the team would not only take part in the teaching process but would evaluate each other. Those who have taken part in the team teaching ministries, either in a secular or religious setting, are quick to agree that the level of teaching has been greatly enhanced by the evaluation process. Even though some people chafe under its practice, they are quick to agree concerning its value. There must always be the cooperative attitude in a team which says, "I've got something to learn from you too."

I deeply appreciate the various members of the body of Christ who have loved me enough to provoke me to good works and to correct me when I have been going in the wrong direction. Team members will be growing in Christ and in turn greatly influencing the Spirit's development of those in their charge as they are involved in this provoking process.

3

Seeing Jesus' Standards

"And Jesus came up and spoke to them saying, 'All authority has been given to Me in heaven and on earth. Go, therefore, and make disciples of all the nations . . . teaching them to observe all that I have commanded you' " (Matt. 28:19-20).

This injunction is to all nations—and often we forget that our nation is included in those commanded to make disciples. The command of Christ is not to go and help people to stockpile religious information so they can make proper creedal statements about their belief in Christ. The goal is to go and *make disciples.*

A disciple is a Christian who desires to obey all that Christ has commanded, which of course necessitates his knowing biblical truths. If you are to judge the success of your Christian education ministry, one of the major criteria will be: Are your students obeying biblical commands?

I have had the opportunity to observe over 2,000 Bible School teachers in their classrooms and to discuss with them their respective ministries. My major concern is that so few teachers are caught up in the process of making disciples; most seem to be satisfied when their students can verbalize religious information.

Christ has given us specific guidelines for ways of teaching the Word of God in the church—just as clearly as He has given us the explicit truths we should teach. I wish we were as concerned about *how* we are to teach as to *what* we are to teach. When God promises to bless His Word, that clearly means He will also bless effective methods for teaching it. And we have not succeeded in our task until we have made disciples.

Christ clearly modeled every life principle which He taught. When He taught His disciples to pray, He gave them a model prayer, and He took them with Him into the mountains for prayer. His disciples looked on as He had spiritual dialogues with needy souls, thus learning firsthand how to witness.

One Sunday evening I sat in a church balcony behind three 8th-grade girls. Their Bible school teacher sat a couple of rows in front of them. It was obvious that he was unaware the girls from his class were seated behind him because he read his Sunday School paper instead of listening to the pastor's message. They laughed about what they saw. In one church service the teacher negated the lesson which he had taught them earlier on giving attention to the Word of God. You can imagine how this bad example multiplied the teacher's obstacles to effective communication,

Christ was well aware that His students would not learn a truth until they integrated it into their actions. When Christ taught the need for humility, He modeled that truth by washing His disciples' fee. Every truth which I see Christ teaching is inculcated by a careful plan to have His students involved with that truth in their lives. Yet in my observation of Sunday School teachers, I have found only a handful making plans to involve their students in a learning activity that embodies the specific truth they are teaching.

A high school teacher was teaching a lesson about temptation to sin. He was anxious that his students first become aware of the constant bombardment of so many subtle temptations, so he provided a wrist-worn golf score counter which they could click each time they were confronted with a satanic device for getting them off of God's path. Of course, the teacher also stressed the nature of temptation and Christ's ability to overcome its lure. By engaging his students in life-activated learning, the teacher was transforming words into conduct.

Other biblical methods for teaching the Word of God could be listed, such as emphasizing the Bible as the constant teacher, not the person leading the class. We often hear teachers offering opinions and answers when students might better turn to the Word of God to discover and explore the truth God has given.

Another "method" God promises to bless is the disciple maker's or teacher's purity of life. This method may be completely overlooked by teachers favoring an exciting atmosphere and the latest dynamic teaching tools.

We are told in Colossians 1:28 that the objective of teaching is to "present every man complete in Christ." This refers to maturity, or being fully taught or godly, in contrast to being a novice in faith and life. Christ's teaching about discipleship stresses loving obedience in passages like John 14:23. "If anyone loves Me, he will keep My Word." It's the response to His words that makes the decisive difference.

This same emphasis regarding God's commandments, statutes, and judgments was stressed by Moses, so the people of God "might do them in the land." Our teaching cannot afford to seek less. A true test of effective teaching is to see if we are achieving behavioral objectives.

It's thrilling to hear an adult class member discuss with another member how a Bible lesson was put into practice. This develops through a different emphasis than learning the content of a chapter.

An adult class studied the necessity of the body of Christ

being a caring community, and the teacher read two newspaper articles from that week's paper about two local families who had experienced a tragedy. He asked for two couples to take the names and visit to see what the class might do to meet their needs. That's learning the Bible lesson of the week!

I believe Christ also showed us the value of small-group discipleship, where sharing, involvement, and various provocative experiences can take place. When a Christian becomes a committed saint, he should be introduced to a group where this can occur. Especially where the master-teacher approach in large classes is used, some provision needs to be made for involvement with others in learning and living the Word of God.

These illustrations show that it is easy to deviate from biblical methods for teaching the Word of God. We must constantly use self and group analysis to keep us from slipping away from the guidelines our Lord has given us. Many Sunday Schools and individual teachers have moved away from the biblical blueprint through a desire to be contemporary. We must be up-to-date in applications and insights, but we must remember that it is possible to teach false doctrine by not being an honest student of the Word of God.

Hopefully, you are ready now to conduct an evaluation, and you are convinced of the necessity to be continually involved in an evaluation program. Scripture gives us criteria by which to evaluate our effectiveness, but since each individual Sunday School is uniquely designed and exists in its own unique cultural setting, additional interpretations of the guidelines are needed for each case. An agreed job description or standard of competency is absolutely essential. If you are not ready to adopt a formulated definition of a competent school and teacher, your staff should do some serious planning.

Dr. James Carpenter of Arizona State University has worked with hundreds of public school districts across America to help them define a competent public school teacher. His program, IOTA (Instrument for the Observation of Teaching Activities), is an extremely efficient tool to define a competent teacher. "The Christian Leader" is the spiritual counterpart of IOTA, also designed by Dr. Carpenter, a committed Christian.

His definition of the seven areas of competency are expanded under these titles: (1) disciple maker, (2) counselor, (3) manager of instruction, (4) catalyst in society, (5) interpreter to the community, (6) staff participant, (7) member of a ministry. I recommend participation in his Christian Leader workshops when possible.*

While traveling across the country on a train, I talked with a junior high Sunday School teacher who described at great length how meaningful his class had been to him. After an extended description of his boys, he excitedly concluded: "A year ago I started the class with 16 boys and I still have 8 of them left!"

I appreciated his enthusiasm, but suspected that something else was lacking. Even enthusiasm is missing with some teachers who want to quit because they feel they have not been a success. For both types of teachers, the teaching standard (or lack of one) may be largely at fault.

A standard is a written guide or measure to help maintain excellence in the operation of the Christian education program. It is a target for the workers to aim at. A covenant, on the other hand, is a signed agreement between the church and the teacher specifying their commitments in their joint service to God. A covenant is a promise of performance to Christ and also to the local body of Christ's church.

A standard or a covenant should clarify what is expected of the workers in the school in regard to (1) life-changing

---

*Center for Improvement of Instruction and Learning, P.O. Box 163, Tempe, Arizona 85281.

teaching objectives, (2) regularity and longevity of teaching, (3) efficiency of their work, (4) cooperation with leaders, (5) curriculum and program. Since a biblical principle for a church covenant is that it be autonomously developed, I recommend that a Sunday School covenant be formed by the entire staff under the title: "What God Expects of Me." Its demands must be reasonable enough to be met by the signers, and there must be no discrepancy between the real objectives and the tests used to measure their achievement.

There is always a danger that a standard or covenant might promote a legalistic attitude. The standards themselves never become legalistic, but the attitude of workers who lose sight of the spiritual objectives can become rigidly mechanical or aridly critical of others. The standard remains a worthy instrument in discipleship.

You may confront another major objection to the development and use of a covenant in the assertion that each Christian is a priest who is responsible to God alone. As far as our individual life is concerned, that is true; but in our service with and to the body of Christ, we are responsible also to these members of the body. A covenant covers our action in the fulfillment of specific, regular tasks with the body. Its lofty goal inevitably heightens our performance.

4
Tracing Your Profile

I heard about a lady who won't turn on the light when she's fixing her hair in front of the mirror. She's afraid she won't be able to endure seeing the wrinkles lining her face. She hopes she'll be able to make herself presentable by just fixing the outline of her flowing hair reflected in the mirror.

A lot of people look at their church's ministry in the same way. They don't want to investigate too closely for fear they might see organizational cracks and personnel blemishes. But will keeping the lights low fool anyone? Not the visitor with an unmet need. Not the all-seeing God. Remember that when you turn on the bright lights you see the beauty to rejoice in as well as the blemishes which need healing.

In order to grow, we have to be willing to "lean into the pain" of stretching. Churches, like people, do not grow when they ignore their deficiencies. A school with a full complement of teachers may be grievously failing its objectives. What's really happening in these classrooms and in the lives of students is the measure of the ministry.

Since administrative decisions are usually based on observed conditions, we dare not make any decisions, large or small, without knowing what the conditions actually are. This requires evaluation to be a continual process, not a once-a-year project. If workers are convinced that the evaluation increases their effectiveness and strengthens the overall ministry of the church, they will more readily participate in the evaluation process.

Drawing an accurate profile of your church's educational program is the first step in determining the effectiveness of your school. This means you will draw detailed word-pictures which show your school close-up.

In recent years a number of programs have been developed to assist churches in compiling a profile of their congregations. The Wesleyan Sunday School Department (Box 2000, Marion, Ind. 46952) developed a tool called the Clinical Evaluation Program. A number of other denominations have adapted the work of Dr. Willard Harly, Jr. to their own situations. In this program all the congregation members answer 150 questions about the way they respond to their church's ministry. The computer digests the information and produces an extensive report comprising 22,000 pieces of information.

Research analyst Dr. James Engel of Wheaton College (Wheaton, Ill. 60187) has refined methods for tabulating the pulsebeats of congregations. The Christian education department of the Horn Creek Conference Grounds in Westcliff, Colorado, has developed a method. The Southern Baptist Convention (127 9th Avenue N, Nashville, Tenn. 37234) offers a comprehensive, helpful packet to aid a church in self-analysis. Such organizations as the Church Growth Services (120 Callandor St., South Bend, Ind., 46614) provide professional aid in developing a church profile as a means to determine the kind of facilities needed to minister to growing congregations.

The developing profile should include three basic parts: (1) a historical profile of the church's educational program; (2) a community profile; and (3) a ministry profile. Here we will talk about these kinds of information to secure, and in the next chapter the instruments needed to gather the information.

1. A Historical Profile

You cannot draw an exact profile of what your church history has been, but by gathering sufficient data you will visualize the outlines of the Christian education ministries and perceive some of the major influences shaping their impact. Though you are not primarily interested in the number of people involved, a study of the attendance changes can give a clue to the spiritual vitality of the congregation. A church that has not kept accurate attendance records will be hampered in making projections toward the future. A church should keep records of each class and department, plus its total attendance and enrollment. With these records for reference, you can develop the following graphs:

    a. A 10-year study of the monthly average attendance of each class

    b. A 10-year study of the monthly average attendance of each department

    c. A 10-year study showing the total average attendance of the Sunday School

    d. A graph showing comparisons between the yearly average enrollment and the yearly average attendance of the school

    e. A graph showing comparisons for the last 10 years of the average Sunday School attendance with the average morning worship service

    f. Graphs depicting the attendance of various clubs and youth programs conducted within the Christian education framework

When the graphs are completed, you are ready to translate your findings. A difficult but meaningful step at this time is to interpret the rise and falls in your various graphs. You'll want to determine the effect that various staff people have had on attendance trends. Note the effect, if any, of attendance contests and special days on enrollment. What part has disciplined or casual leadership played in attendance figures? When was a calling program vigorous or apathetic?

You no doubt will be able to correlate various spiritual highs and lows with the attendance records. You may be able to link special evangelism efforts, the number of people brought to Christ, and how many joined the church. As you connect historical events with the graphs, you can estimate the effectiveness of some programs conducted in the past. Both attendance gains and slumps can help you focus on causes that are important to your ministry.

An evaluation of your facilities is vital to the extension of your educational program.

Dr. Richard Meyers (Religious Research Center, 4821 Carvel Avenue, Indianapolis, Ind. 46205) discovered through extensive research on the factors of church growth, that the attractiveness of the rooms, the furniture, the lighting, and the ventilation definitely affect the people who attend. His statistics reinforced the old maxim, "A group will never outgrow its facilities." In other words, if a room will comfortably accommodate 10 people, it is futile to hope that 10 people will jam in regularly. Furthermore, a room used by several groups will tend to diminish the size of any one group meeting there.

Dr. Lawrence Richards in *The Key to Sunday School Achievement* (Moody Press) provides a key to ideal department size and equipment needs. As you make careful projections for growth at your church, this guide can help you make a judicious facility-need protection.

When your historical profile is completed, you will have insights into how many teachers you should recruit and train for the coming year. The space needed and the material to be ordered will also be indicated.

A few years ago I was asked to do an evaluation study of a particular church. After I had completed the 10-year graph, I discovered an interesting phenomenon. For the first five years of that period the pastor was a moderately effective pulpiteer who put a great deal of effort into the development of the Sunday School, causing both ministries to grow. When he left, the church called a pastor with a reputation for preaching skill. He chose not to emphasize the Sunday School, and during the next five years both the Sunday School and the church service declined in attendance. It was obvious to me that the Sunday School was a very influential factor in the life of that church. These are the kinds of things that can be discovered by a thorough look at your historical profile.

2. Community Profile (see Appendix, page 117-"Record of Attendance")

The congregation of a large church used a huge map of their city to identify their individual residences with colored pins. These neighborhoods became areas for which they felt a special responsibility. Such an identification helped particularize their community profile.

To help you draw a profile of your community, visit the city hall, county court house, school board office, or the Chamber of Commerce office to seek various information about the people where you live. Age of people is one factor. When you have ascertained the number in each age bracket, calculate the percentage of each group to the overall population, then compare the proportions with these age groups in your congregation. A large discrepancy may signal your need to shift efforts and programs in new directions. The same is true regarding other factors.

A large inner-city church striving to build a strong children's department was totally frustrated. After preparing a community profile, they realized the changing community was burgeoning with senior citizens. Though they continued to operate a children's department, a major thrust toward older people not only expanded the church but deepened its effectiveness in the community.

Each community has a distinctive personality, though embracing many diverse characteristics. An honest study of your community profile will prevent you from confusing your church with other churches and will help you to make keener decisions about your program emphasis for the future.

3. Ministry Profile

Gathering the data in this area will be much more difficult than the previous two. Here you will be looking for information concerning the effectiveness of evangelism, nurture, and service in your educational program. All three of these must be evaluated specifically as they apply to the student. Make certain that this is done on the basis of fact-finding and not fault-finding. Be as objective as possible, and draw conclusions which are clearly verified by facts.

A basic requirement for this part of the evaluation is to know specifically the objectives of your Sunday School. Keep in mind that the effectiveness of teachers is proportional to the degree they have made the goals of the school their own. There is a strong tendency to evaluate the school in relation to its events and activities rather than its purpose and goals. And there is a common impulse to hand down the goals formed by the leaders rather than letting the workers discuss and shape them. This time-consuming process insures much deeper commitment by the workers to the overall goals of the Sunday School.

The kinds of things you are going to try to identify in the ministry profile are as follows:

- intensity of teachers' involvement with students
- spiritual vitality of the staff
- effectiveness of the curriculum
- effectiveness of its use
- extensiveness of staff training
- how grouping and grading are handled
- cooperation between the church and Sunday School
- level of proficiency in the teaching/learning process used by the staff
- kind of discipline used and how effectively it is practiced
- type of evangelistic outreach practiced
- effectiveness of communication among all staff members
- efficiency of staff members in following through with responsibilities
- kind of equipment used in the teaching ministry
- Availability of visual aids and reading aids for teachers

No doubt you will want to add some items of special importance to your situation. Now, let's look at the instruments used in gleaning this invaluable information.

5
Shaping Your Tools

An elderly gentleman was given a report from the doctor in the emergency room at the hospital, and he was extremely pleased to hear that his heart was in perfect condition. Not until the next day was he informed that the wrong testing machine was used. His blood pressure was up to par, but his heart condition left much to be desired. You might get a very satisfactory report on the vitality of your church educational program, but you must be sure you have used the right instrument.

The proper instrument for testing can be developed only when you have in writing the exact objective you are checking. The more precisely your objectives are defined, the more accurately you can measure accomplishments.

There is no end to the various types of instruments which are available for testing. Our plan is to help you develop your own and to include a couple of samples in the process so you can accurately test your self-chosen objectives. The completed evaluation should be tested on a small group of people to make sure it measures the qualities in question. You may need to alter and refine some points before printing the final copy.

The following guidelines give practical suggestions for developing your evaluation instrument. Careful design will avoid indefinite and perhaps even faulty results.

1. Since the instrument should test the fulfillment of the job description for various workers, and an adequate job description for teachers specifies what kind of growth ought to occur in students, the instrument must include examination of students to see if their lives are growing as a result of their Sunday School involvement.

2. Give opportunity to report both healthy and unhealthy practices, or positive as well as negative results. Since workers should be complimented on areas of efficiency, these competencies must be known to be commended.

3. Where teachers may express negative feelings on a point, give occasion for expressing the reason. For example, if some teachers will indicate they fail to arrive 15 minutes before starting time, they should have an opportunity on the following question to check a multiple choice somewhat as follows:

   _____ My family hinders me.
   _____ I pick up riders.
   _____ I don't think it's important.
   _____ I don't plan my time right.
   _____ Other reason (specify). _ _____

4. Allow plenty of latitude for free, accurate responses. In some sections it is appropriate to include an open question to cover a significant aspect you cannot specify.

5. When you plan to tabulate the results, list objective choices that can be systematically counted. Subjective —individualistic—answers are nearly impossible to tabulate. For example, in framing a question concerning the amount of training attained, the answers specify a range of choices to fit all possibilities.

Mv training and teaching techniques include:

1. One course   _____
2. Two or more courses   _____
3. On-the-job training   _____
4. None   _____

6. If you are asking for such things as attendance or population lists, or percentages of items, it is wise to leave sufficient spaces for all the separate numbers (see Record of Attendance in Appendix).

7. When you sense an important question may be misunderstood or the blunt truth may be hard to admit, try framing two questions on the same topic. If one question fails to yield the information you seek (or there is some doubt about its accuracy), the two questions may be checked against each other (this is much easier if computer analysis is used). When asked if a lesson usually feeds a student spiritually, for instance, the first response may yield a low mark. Yet a second question, such as the following, may shed a different light.

My spiritual growth through Sunday School can be defined as:

_____ becoming less interested

_____ reading my Bible more

_____ praying more

_____ changing attitudes

_____ growing dedication to Christ

_____ growing spiritual interest

_____ witnessing more

8. Place the logical answer in a multiple-choice series low in the list. People have a strong tendency to mark the earlier choices in a list if they are careless or are uncertain about the question.

1. Leaders' Evaluation (see Pastor and General Superintendent evaluation form in Appendix, page 86)

Since a leader's responsibility covers wide areas, it is important to get information about each one, especially those covered in their job descriptions. Some sample information goals:

A. How do they handle their administrative tasks?

B. How do they show care for the ultimate fulfillment of their goals in the lives of students in their program?

C. How competent are they in handling personnel under their leadership? This would include recruitment, training, and encouragement of those workers.

D. Look for signs in their administration which indicate the use of initiative and planning—how effective have they been in following up programs which they have initiated?

E. How much care have they given to record-keeping and the utilization of those facts?

F. How well do they keep open the lines of communication to those for whom they are accountable?

A wisely planned instrument provides opportunities for leaders to share insights into why they have succeeded or failed. For instance, you may ask how many staff meetings have been held and also the type of agenda followed and the kind of publicity given the meetings. Further questions might probe whether the meetings were regularly scheduled, or whether they had more to do with business than training. The teacher's form may inquire whether these meetings fulfilled needs or had other drawbacks such as schedule conflicts.

2. Teachers' Evaluations (see Appendix, pg. 98)

It is important here to allow the teachers or workers to judge their own effectiveness. This will lessen the pressure on the person conducting the evaluation. One of the meaningful ways to accomplish this is to provide two different forms. The first would ask teachers to describe an ideal worker or teacher in a number of areas of work. The same question would be reworded on the second form and the teacher would express his actual practices. The workers thus judge themselves, and correction may come much quicker because they have discovered their own weaknesses rather than having someone else judge them.

The following two questions seek to determine the type of involvement teachers have with their students outside the class. First they are asked to mark their idea of *Establishing A Standard* (see Appendix, pg. 93).

Generally my private discussions with my students after class or during the week deal with:

    a. factual content of Bible lessons taught currently
    b. items of miscellaneous interest only
    c. their attendance at church or sunday School
    d. their class behavior
    e. the practical application of the current lesson to aid their relationship to and growth in Christ.

The same list on the *Teacher Evaluation* would be listed under the question:

Generally my private discussions with my students after class or during the week deal with:

    (Here they would have to give recognition to the fact that they ought to become involved with their students in relation to the lesson taught, but would often indicate that the majority of their contacts were simply in relation to absenteeism. This would greatly encourage them to change their involvement with their students.)

To obtain further insights into a teacher's competence you'd be able to glean a great deal of insight into a teacher's behavior by checking other questions related to that subject. For instance, you might discover that a teacher is only spending an hour and a half in preparation each week. In some cases that would be sufficient, but you might notice on that same teacher's questionnaire that he has no training in teaching technique and that he generally uses only two methods of teaching. You may also discover that he has no involvement with his students, uses very few multimedia, and does not ask his students to become involved in learning activities. (A teacher who is proficient in all those other areas might be able to accomplish a great deal in an hour and a half of preparation time.)

You would not be greatly concerned if a teacher was not instrumental in introducing any of his students to Christ if he is speaking personally to all his students about Christ, or in class has registered the fact that he has already made a decision for Christ. On the other hand, we would be greatly concerned if there were no decisions and no efforts were made to introduce students to a personal commitment to Christ.

There are two basic ways to glean information about the teacher's performance. Either let him report what is happening in his ministry as has just been explained, or let another person observe what he does. The latter tends to be rather threatening to many workers. The *Observation Evaluation Sheet* on page 81 in the Appendix is designed to overcome that kind of pressure. The teacher and the evaluator are both familiar with the instrument. They study and discuss beforehand what competence entails. The evaluator simply writes down in each appropriate box on the instrument what he sees happening (how many times the students participate; the condition of the room; how many learning activities were involved; what materials are used; etc.). The evaluator simply writes his observations. He lets the teacher make the judgment about the positive or negative effectiveness.

The form on page 82 of the Appendix, *Evaluation of the Teaching/Learning Process,* is another way to glean that data.

This, too, should be studied by both evaluator and teacher *beforehand*. Don't plan on using this unless you will be discussing the marked form with the teacher after the class. It provides a unique help for the teacher to improve his teaching.

3. Students' Evaluation (see Appendix, page 108)

Most students do not thoroughly understand what a genuine teaching/learning process involves and consequently would find it difficult to judge the competency of their teachers. A student evaluation form can give us a great deal of insight, however, into whether or not the student is growing in Christ as a result of his involvement with the teacher and class. It is recognized that junior high students and younger find it much more difficult to judge the competency of a teaching/learning situation than those in high school and above.

When you ask students to tell how their lives are affected by their involvement in the various Christian education programs, they will produce a tremendous variety of answers. A good way to systematize the problem is to have them mark on a numbered grid. 1 2 3 4 5 6 7 8 This allows them to express their feeling in a range of degrees which can be tabulated. The total should be even numbered rather than uneven to avoid "dead-center" answers.

When all of the students and staff members have completed their evaluation forms, it is time to tabulate your findings. In some cases you will get averages, but in most cases you will get totals. You'll want to compare your findings from the *Establishing A Standard* form with the actual performance on their *Teacher Evaluation*.

To get a reading of what is actually occurring in the program, it is extremely important that you get statistics from at least 80% of the workers. You could work from a checklist to insure reaching your quota. (Teachers should not be asked to put their names on their forms.)

Your church and its program are distinct from all others. You needn't have any hesitation about developing your own unique form to test the effectiveness and competency of your program. In fact, the best forms will be those which you develop yourself. But take great care in its formulation so you will get accurate readings of what is occurring. Having tabulated your findings, it is time to plan improvements of your program and staff.

6
Sighting Your Goals

The assistant football coach hurried from the press box where he had observed the game during the first half. His notebook and head were crammed with the action on the field. The strengths and weaknesses of both teams had been checked against the game strategy planned before the encounter, and now it was time to revamp some miscalculations and allow for unforeseen factors. The right plan should insure victory!

Our evaluation process at this point compares with half-time at a football game. Or it is illustrated by the man described in the Book of James who looked in the mirror and discovered his face was dirty (James 1:23). That man is not our model, for he ignored the facts he discovered. Our evaluation project will be a waste of time and energy if you fail to do anything about your findings. You may conclude you need to shift your target, as well as adjust your "shooting stance" so you achieve a higher score in effectiveness.

This step will help you discover if the people on your team are satisfied with the status quo or if they want to be change-agents. Are you genuinely interested in strengthening your ministry? If they are content merely to be critics, they'll stop at this point. But most workers will be happy for an evaluation that is conducted for spiritual growth. Setting goals will give a great sense of encouragement to them. It would be a tragedy not to progress beyond this point, though filling out the questionnaires exposes attitudes and conditions upon which the Holy Spirit can work.

People are more likely to implement goals vigorously when they have had a voice in shaping them. To simply announce at a staff meeting that you have established a goal of seeing that all teachers are more adequately trained during the next year may kill your embryonic plans. Since everyone cannot be involved personally in the development of the goals, you need to see that as many leaders as possible are involved. Then a spirit of teamwork is vital in presenting the goals for adoption.

Many books and articles have been written concerning the development and establishment of goals. I will deal with goal-setting in the light of the evaluation process. An honest and accurate evaluation should reveal the problem areas and specific needs should be written on a worksheet, even though some of them cannot possibly be dealt with at the present time. Unrecorded, they readily are lost. Written down, they guide you in dreaming dreams, focusing your prayers, and keying the agendas for your planning meetings. With such a list, you'll never lack a subject for a staff meeting.

It is important to deal with needs, goals, and strategy step by step. If you jump the step of goals, for example, you might limit your creativity and effectiveness. The evaluation process may reveal that you have a need to give additional training to your staff; that will be written down as a "need." The "strategy" might be to start a teacher training class on Sunday evenings. Not to write down your "goal" at this point may blind you to the possibility that there are many other strategies for training your staff. For instance, it could be done by correspondence, or it might be handled by some outside organization. Or you might develop a LEROY certification program as described in chapter two. Therefore, noting your goal widens your awareness to various possible strategies. A later chapter will present the establishment of varied types of strategy.

Though your goals may look quite similar to those of some other church with which you're familiar, they will be basically different because your church has its own personality and the needs you face stem from that uniqueness. The following points give some guidelines for accurately formulating your goals once you have read your statistics. You will need to read your forms in light of the questions you have designed.

Since it would be frustrating to try to work on all of your goals at once you should establish a list of priorities. The natural chronological sequence and the urgency of various goals will help establish their precedence. Of course, occasional shifts in the order may be advisable as they are implemented, but it is important always to have a workable goal immediately ahead.

Here are some of the things to look for as you study the statistics gathered from your tabulation.

1. The gaps between their ideal established by the teacher and the actual performance will clearly indicate some strong need. Three-fourths of the teachers may indicate they ought to make personal visits in the homes of all of their absentees, while in actuality their *Teacher Evaluation* form indicates that only one-fourth of them are actually making home visits. This directly points out that you must provide some sort of a program to stimulate making those contacts.

2. Compare job descriptions and reports of performance to discover additional areas of need. The job description of the departmental superintendent may call for departmental meetings each month with the report indicating they're only meeting a couple of times a year. If Sunday School teachers feel the need for

departmental meetings, you'll add to your list of needs the goal to conduct departmental staff meetings.

3. In a study of the *Student Questionnaires* you may find that lessons for life-changing behavioral objectives are not being applied by the students. They may indicate that they are not implementing Scripture into their daily lives. Plan to incorporate this step into your school's improvement by adding it to your list of needs and goals.

4. As you study the attendance percentage of each department, compare them with the percentage of that same age-bracket in your community profile. A careful study here leads you to see whether some age-group ought to receive more attention in your outreach.

5. A careful study of all the figures from your attendance charts should help you establish a projected growth figure. From those figures you should be able to determine how many additional staff people should be needed and how many additional rooms should be provided for the coming year. For instance, you would want to plan for an additional teacher for every ten pupils you anticipate adding to your roll.

6. Since relationships are a major part of the church's ministry, you should give serious consideration to the interplay of all of your personnel. This would include the administrative staff with the various workers as well as the relationships among the teachers, workers, and the students. For instance, if the students feel the teachers are not deeply concerned about their spiritual well-being, some significant steps should be taken to improve those relationships.

7. Discuss with workers the findings from your various studies. They will be able to help interpret the data, which of course will reveal other needs and problems.

The more clearly a goal is defined, the greater will be the possibility of fulfilling it. Here are some guidelines to assist you in formulating them.

    a. Be specific. Make certain that the goal spells out explicitly what is to be accomplished, who is to implement the action, and what data is set for its accomplishment.

    b. Be realistic. Make certain the goals are within the reach of the people involved. You cannot set a goal for the Holy Spirit to accomplish, but you can set a goal which would specify the accomplishments of the personnel involved. It is not wise to say that you will expect so many converts in a period of time, but it is realistic to say you expect a certain number of witnessing contacts during that period. Do not plan so small that the people are not stretched; they may need to hurt a bit in order to accomplish the goals. An unreasonable goal, however, will discourage your personnel at the beginning.

    c. Set goals commensurate with the current abilities of your people. If your teachers lack the know-how to help students make a decision for Christ, the priority goal may be for training rather than appointments for witnessing.

    d. Check to see that goals are compatible with overall objectives. Aim for your people to be involved with goals that will help to bring your people to "maturity in Jesus Christ."

    e. Fashion goals that are clearly meaningful. Each person should understand why the goal in which he is involved is important. Why should he be turning out such a great effort? Practical and significant helpfulness to people must be evident.

    f. Define goals so they are measurable. The participants need to see when they have reached their goal. One way to test the writing of a goal is to see if it fits within the framework of this statement: "Hey, Dad, I can _____." Is it that specific? If so, then no doubt it is measureable. Also, see that accountability is built into this part of the goal as well.

You might write a goal specifying that each teacher should visit each absentee who has been absent three or more Sundays. To encourage each teacher in following through, have them fill out a report on their calls, helping them to be accountable for the task.

When your goals are established, and you see clearly the direction you need to move during the months ahead, you are ready to establish strategy to help you fulfill those meaningful objectives.

7

Planning
Your Strategies

One way to look at your leadership task is to illustrate the job that needs to be done as a brick that must be moved from position 'A' to position 'B'. If you're ever going to get it there, it's going to take more than just thinking about it. It means getting it in motion. Maybe it's going to mean some hard work. There may be some detours around which you'll have to work. *Strategy*—the key word at this point simply means finding a way to move the brick from position 'A' to position 'B' which will get it to its destination most rapidly with the least amount of effort.

Here are four basic rules to keep in mind as you think about designing and implementing your strategy:

1. "Good goals are my goals and bad goals are your goals" is a psychological fact of life. We feel most responsible for those things that we have had a part in generating. It is only logical that the first law of discipline is identical to the first law of implementing strategy: People must have a say in the policy which regulates them.

A worker's self-guided contract was discussed at the conclusion of Chapter Two. This is one way to implement this principle. The worker has a say in the kind of goals he is to work toward, and he can help design his own program and strategy for accomplishing the goals he designed.

2. Devise strategy that will meet your needs and fulfill your goals as closely as possible. If you had walked into the president's office of a leading railroad 75 years ago and asked what the railroad was doing, probably he would say, "We are running our railroad." Twenty-five years ago you would probably have heard the same answer. Today the railroad would likely say, "We are trying to avoid bankruptcy."

If 25 years ago you had asked the president of IBM what his company was doing, he might have said they were busily involved in tabulating information for humans. Since you had just toured their large factories, you might question his answer because you noticed they were manufacturing computers. If you had challenged his answer, he might wisely have said, "We just happen to be making computers because they provide the best means we know now to compile and process data for human beings." Someone has wisely suggested that if the railroads had been concentrating on transporting people some years ago perhaps today they would be running not only the railroads but the airlines as well.

Schools face the same problem. It is tempting to concentrate on the machinery of an organization and forget the purpose of the machinery. Sunday Schools are to bring people to maturity in Christ, but many schools are satisfied to operate a system. They move fewer and fewer people to stopover points instead of increasing numbers to the destination.

Strategy, therefore, must contain or allow for flexibility. It must also include constant review to see if strategy is suited to the goals. In the next chapter we will talk in detail about specific strategies designed to meet goals.

A creative administrator will observe many other churches' program designs to gain ideas. He will see that others' programs will not work in the same way in his situation, but he will adapt some devices which will help him accomplish his objectives. He reminds himself as well as co-workers that his strategies are simply means to accomplish vital ends. This means they can be scrapped or modified whenever they are not helping to meet those objectives.

When a person gets a vision for a mighty work, he sees his goal way out in the distant horizon. In order to move from his vision to his objective he needs a serviceable vehicle—a program or strategy. Sometimes the vision has faded because it is far past, the goal is still a speck on the horizon, and we creatures of the present are preoccupied with the things surrounding us. Consequently we often lose sight of both the vision and the objective.

A church had a keen desire for their teachers to minister in depth to all the students on their roll. This became increasingly difficult when many became irregular. The school designed a program for contacts of absentees. Each teacher was to send a card after the first absence, make a phone call after the second absence, and visit in person after three consecutive absences. But the strategy-vehicle degenerated through expediencies so departmental secretaries and superintendents were making the contacts. Thus the teachers dispensed truth on Sundays and canceled their opportunities to exhibit the Christ-modeled life during the week. The substitute contacts were genuine but inevitably less effective in reaching the goal of improved attendance.

3. Any idea worth developing must be assigned to a specific person with a time and place for initiation and termination, and the designation of a person to whom he will be accountable. Don't end a planning meeting without making these assignments.

You will seldom find a growing, progressive church that does not have a complete planning calendar. Usually the calendars are developed six months to a year in advance. A useful calendar may list not only the events to be held but the days when the preparations begin.

You can plan into your year's calendar the programs that will help you meet your observable objectives. For instance, you might counter a chronic tardiness problem among your congregation. One church planned a whole month to work on the problem by starting an "early-bird club." They commended and highlighted the on-time people each Sunday with an "early bird" ribbon and emphasized their cooperation and diligence.

4. The power and efficient use of any athletic instrument, such as a baseball bat or a golf club, depends greatly on the follow-through. This is true also for implementation of any kind of strategy.

Everyone seems to make better progress when he has voluntarily made himself accountable to someone else. The concept of discipleship is based on this principle, and it is strategically important in accomplishing our objectives in the church of Jesus Christ. In organizational activities it works not only when the leader invites co-workers to share in setting their own goals, but when the leader asks team members to hold him accountable for his own goals.

Voluntary accountability is potent because it strengthens the caring-relationship between individuals. It demonstrates the importance of one's efforts to another. The lack of follow-through attention causes many workers to slacken their endeavors or quit altogether. We are bombarded by so many demands and tempting diversions that we have a subconscious way of measuring the importance of tasks by how much interest others show in them. Accountability is a great way to express our interest in others. The follow-up must not fail on the designated date, nor can appreciative interest be forgotten.

Assigning intermediate checkpoints in advance will help workers to recover lost ground if something goes amiss in the early stages. These are especially helpful in major or complex assignments.

Here is an example of a carefully designed strategy-follow-up plan. Every Sunday morning the departmental secretary fills out in triplicate the list of each teacher's absentees for the day. The list includes the number of weeks absent. The second copy goes to the general superintendent and the third to the departmental superintendent. Beside each name is a space for the teacher to report the kind of contact made with the absent student during the week.

As the superintendent's major concern is the spiritual development of every student and he cannot personally follow up every student, he assigns teachers who work under his supervision to do that task. He knows that each student must be involved with the teachers in the Word of God and in personal association if they are to grow in Christ. The teachers know the departmental superintendent and the general superintendent will be checking every Sunday to see if they have made a contact of concern. If a form is not returned by the teacher, the departmental superintendent inquires about any difficulty. The check reminds the teachers that personal concern for a student is of utmost importance in teaching the Word of God and thus making disciples. Often Sunday Schools fail to minister to wayward students because superintendents do not follow through with their team of teachers.

The next chapter describes other strategies that churches have found successful in strengthening and enlarging their Christian education ministries.

8
Savoring Success

In our day you can't help but think and talk about success. You can be sure many people in your church view the concept as some kind of magical necessity in life. Our era may be classified as the golden age of the salesman since we stress the number of items sold, produced, and acquired. Of course, quantity is not completely foreign to the New Testament. A study of Acts and Ephesians gives us the impression that Christ wanted the church to grow in quantity as well as quality.

As you evaluate your church, be sure to do so in the light of the specific goals you have established. If you don't keep definite goals before the people, they will set their own goals and judge the Sunday School's success by the secondary, uncoordinated objectives. Of course, you are not going to judge your success only in light of numerical growth; increasing competence and strengthening lives in Jesus Christ are the ultimate goal. When churches are concerned about both their quantitative and qualitative growth, the long-range effect of their ministry is much greater. Qualitative goals advance quantitative goals, and numerical aspects contribute to the overall maturity of your school.

Many congregations are reluctant to take strategic steps because they fear they will take the wrong ones. The greater danger is that a church takes no significant steps at all, and evident problems continue unattended. Though the strategy you choose may not be the best possible, it will accomplish God's work if undertaken prayerfully and diligently.

Following are brief accounts of churches that have chosen a vehicle and moved into action. Their efforts have proven successful in fulfilling those quantitative-qualitative objectives they set for themselves.

One of the major purposes of the Conservative Baptist Association of America's computerized evaluation program called Church Profile seeks to uncover four major needs of a congregation. Every study seems to have revealed that one of the basic needs was for close intimate relationship among its members. These churches have adopted varied strategies to meet that need. Some have developed care groups among their adult classes in their Sunday School. They say the ideal size in each group is from four to twelve people. These members learn to practice intimate care for the other members of their cell group.

They might help meet a material need. They definitely pray for each other regularly. During the week or in class they discuss the life-changing responses called for by their Sunday School lesson. One teacher set up the classroom with a number of tables at which the same cell-group members gathered each week to discuss the lesson and interact with each other. Churches and classes using this method find there is a more meaningful relationship among members of the group and consequently the group tends to grow in size.

Another study of a Sunday School disclosed the pupils were slow in putting into action the specific truths taught in Sunday School (not that this was a surprise!). Since this problem concerned a majority of the teachers, a series of lessons for the

Sunday School staff was designed to help. As techniques were explained in a staff meeting, teachers were asked to develop and use a new truth in class the following Sunday. At the next departmental meeting, their progress or failure was discussed. This built team spirit among the staff as well as helping teachers to relate the truth to their students.

It was discovered in one church that one third of the teachers were consistently using only three teaching techniques. As a result, a series of staff meetings were prepared to demonstrate additional techniques. Dr. Kenneth Gangel's book *Twenty-Four Ways To Improve Your Teaching* was a helpful tool in summarizing methods for variety and effectiveness. Each teacher was asked to use at least one new method in the coming month. Afterward he was to explain his success and express his difficulties at the next staff meeting.

Space problems are often divulged in a proper analysis of a Sunday School. Churches have discovered that the size of their rooms seems to be increased by carpeting the floors. Heavy drapes or carpet added to the walls not only enhance the beauty of the room but improve the accoustical properties of the room. Sometimes this encourages changes toward open-classroom teaching which utilizes many of the features of team teaching. This allows churches to expand the pupil-teacher ratio by adding many more study units in the same amount of floor space.

One church discovered that its Adult Department attendance was declining because of decreased interest and meaningfulness. A crash teachers' training program was put in gear for one quarter to raise competence. Within six months after the training course the Adult Department doubled in size.

A small church of about 50 people found their adult class of 10 struggling to push beyond that mark. Once in a while it reached 12. Various people came and went but the class did not grow. Who would dare start another class when one couldn't thrive? The superintendent noticed two young couples who were not attending Sunday School. After consultation, he asked one man in the struggling class to start a new class for young adults. Within a month that class had grown to 12, while the previous class continued with 10. Apparently the strategy-vehicle was the right one to implement the goal of building the adult department.

Often when a church institutes a bus program, a great influx of students with little biblical background puts special strains on teachers and regular pupils. The teaching process is jumbled, and some students drop out in frustration. One church boldly instituted a basic-Christianity class. The church appointed competent teachers both in the Primary and Junior Departments to conduct eight sessions on a continual cycle. No matter when a new student arrived, he got on the track at any one of the eight "stations" and continued until he had covered all eight units. At that time he was moved to the class for the appropriate age.

The foundational class exposed beginning students to the concept of the church, Bible authorship, the role of the Word of God, the persons of the Trinity, and the way of salvation. Other churches have found great benefits through this plan to the students as well as the teachers faithfully conducting their classes.

Another church staff discovered after starting an elective program in their Adult Department that they were losing many members, though others who had not attended previously began to come. The strategy in this case was to make a master roll of all the adults in the church and compare the total adult attendance in Sunday School. It is so easy for adults who switch from one class to the other to soon be lost in the shuffle. An Adult Department secretary gave the name of each inactive adult to the elective classes for follow-up. Some adults never responded, but a number of inactive ones did because of the attention shown them. The strategy produced growth in several directions.

One Sunday School staff recorded a major objective as the evangelizing of people on the attendance roll plus their neighborhood prospects. To their dismay, the evaluation showed that only three of their 21 teachers talked with students about their need for Christ during the preceding year, yet 18 of the teachers stated they did not believe that all of their students knew Christ as Saviour. Once the leadership was aware of this, they made a concerted effort to get the entire Sunday School staff to talk with each one of their students about salvation. Staff meetings included some biblical instruction plus some role plays on evangelism at different age levels. Members came back to the following staff meeting to report the results. It was thrilling to relate that a number of students accepted Christ through this new evangelistic thrust.

A number of churches became concerned that their Sunday School appeared to be mostly a maintenance school rather than an outreach school—this means they are simply maintaining a program for those who choose to come rather than seeking to attract new students. Dissatisfied, they designed strategies to make their program more fruitful within and more far reaching outside. They inaugurated such things as developing Sunday School standards or job descriptions which included teacher follow-up; outreach Cradle Rolls and mothers' clubs which met periodically to touch new homes; neighborhood Bible clubs to draw women to Christ; classes for special groups of people such as the physically handicapped, emotionally disadvantaged, blind, deaf, divorced, senior citizens, and professional workers.

It is not necessary to create a program or strategy which is brand new and spectacular. It is important to find means to move your "brick" from here to there. Seldom do you see a weak church that is striving to provide the basic spiritual essentials and is instituting new programs to meet new needs.

It is true that God's work does not depend *only* on us, but He does ask us to labor in partnership with Him—and to rejoice in the fruit of service done according to His will and in the power of the Holy Spirit.

9

Following Laws to Abundant Grace

Through the 200-year history of the Sunday School movement, certain principles have played significant roles in making impacts on communities. These proven guidelines relate to both quantitative and qualitative growth. Note the interrelatedness of the two types of "laws." No single law will produce the growth you desire. And a law must be put in practice in the proper place to be effective.

We must always be careful that our quest for growth is not motivated by a desire for human honor or the self-seeking manipulation of people. Rather, we are to engage in Sunday School building, as all other things, "heartily, as for the Lord" (Col. 3:23).

I. **Laws Relating Primarily to Quantitative Growth**

A basic guide to Sunday School growth has been developed from observing typical evangelical churches across America. These "laws" have been tested by time and experience.

First Law: A new worker increases attendance by ten. Most Sunday Schools have ten times as many pupils as teachers. The number of teaching centers seem to dictate the attendance. A church with unusual effort may artificially lift its attendance beyond the ratio of ten to one, but will experience a leveling off.

The teacher pupil ratio for the entire Sunday School is about ten to one, but for individual age groups it is different. The average for 4s and 5s is five pupils to one teacher; Primaries, seven to one; Juniors and Junior Highs, nine to one; Young People, thirteen to one; Adults (small churches), fifteen to one; Adults (large churches), twenty-five to one.

Second Law: A class reaches maximum growth in a few months. A new class usually reaches maximum growth in four to eighteen months. Starting new classes rather than expanding present classes is the proved way to build attendance.

Third Law: New classes and departments grow faster, win more people to the Lord, and provide more workers. The truth of "divide to multiply" is pointed out by this law. Teacher training is demanded by this law. Classes cannot be begun without teachers. The pathway to permanent attendance gains is to provide a trained teacher and let the teacher provide the new pupils.

Fourth Law: Age provides the proper basis for division. Pupils of the same age must be placed together for effective teaching. Grading by age locates the responsibility for each period of life and overcomes neglected spans of life. Grading prevents teacher-centered classes. When two ages are placed in the same class, one age eventually tends to be eliminated. Exceptions to the rule might come among adults and also in specialized classes.

Fifth Law: Promotion recognizes the natural laws of growth and keeps Law Four in operation. Promotion is necessary. (This prevents a static outlook in the Sunday School.) Adults should be considered for promotion; this is very difficult, but not impossible.

Sixth Law: Attendance increases in proportion to visitation. Attendance is increased and maintained in proportion to the number of visits and the number of visitors. It usually takes about eight visits to net one increase in attendance.

The authoritative example of the early Christian church, plus numerous Sunday Schools that have been strengthened and enlarged through visitation, furnish ample precedent for a persistent program. A spiritual concern for men can best be demonstrated through visitation. It gives a lay-centered emphasis, which is scriptural. A student-contact plan with built-in teacher accountability tends to greatly facilitate the outreach program.

Seventh Law: A Sunday School takes the shape of the building. A Sunday School must prepare to grow. An established Sunday School must arrange for new classes to grow as it is difficult for a Sunday School to grow beyond the "capacity load" of its building.

II. Laws Relating Primarily to Qualitative Growth

First Law: Teamwork builds strong Sunday Schools. The more the staff works together as a team, the more productive the school will be in the lives of the students.

Since team members supplement, encourage, and strengthen the efforts of other staff people, it is extremely important that regular staff meetings be held with the departmental teams plus the entire staff for communication, goal-setting, building esprit de corps, planning, and training.

Second Law: Being accountable to one another aids the fulfillment of responsibility. Each staff member who is given a responsibility must be held accountable to a democratic standard and to the persons assigned the responsibility of checking. Body accountability is part of "body life" (Hebrews 10:24-25). (Consider the need for accountability on student contacts plus continual class-room evaluation.)

Third Law: People perform their tasks in proportion to the clarity and personal acceptance of their goals. If members are to function as a team, each one must clearly understand the explicit objectives of the school. Accomplishment will be in proportion to their identification with them. This comes by having a voice in developing them and/or in being totally convinced of their values.

Fourth Law: Discipleship teaching produces mature Christians. Teachers who become personally involved with each student in their relationship to Christ and His Word, rather than simply causing students to stockpile religious data, are far more apt to help students become mature saints. Genuine Christian discipleship starts in the classroom but is seldom completed there, so contact students in the home because:
• shepherd-teachers need to give personal guidance;
• concerned teachers check the effect of their teaching;
• friendship establishes better learning;
• contacts show personal interest in the student;
• the student's perceptual mechanism can be ascertained;

- students need personal help to apply the lessons of life;
- biblical values are built through relationships;
- home contacts help assist parents to fulfill their task as family educators;
- you can encourage a decision for Christ;
√ • you can stimulate regular attendance.

Fifth Law: A spiritually and pedagogically-trained staff will best be able to lead students in learning to observe all that the Lord has commanded them (Matt. 28:19-20). Since Christ felt it so critical to train His workers so they would be productive in fruit bearing, how can we expect a harvest without training workers? Not to train them may be asking for failure.

Sixth Law: Students grow spiritually in relation to the quality of the spiritual life of the teacher. One of the major criteria for the selection of staff should be the spiritual quality of their lives. Every effort should be made to facilitate the staff's growth in Christ. A godly teacher keeps watch over the souls of his students in counsel and prayer (Heb. 13:17).

Seventh Law: An adequate conception of God and His Word is greatly benefited by the proper use of the curriculum. A single publishing house's uniform curriculum should be used in the entire school, at least through the youth level, so that each student will have the entire Scripture taught to him in a sequential, orderly way following sound education philosophy. (Exceptions: introductory or special homogeneous classes).

III. Obstructions to Growth

A growing knowledge of the outreach potential demands

an expanding structure and facilities for growth. Ignoring these essential factors confines the process of development of periodic personnel changes and a turnover of adherents; thus, maintaining the *status quo* becomes the norm. Too often churchmen are *content with mediocrity* and settle for *gradualism in growth.* The greater part of all obstructions to the growth process comes from three areas:

conflict of priorities in the lives of personnel;
prison of previous patterns in organization;
limitation of facilities in the building complex.

Know the rules, follow them in love, and abound in fruitful service to God (Phil. 1:9-11).

Appendix

The four Self-Study Guides which follow can be used in numerous ways. Prior to the teachers' developing their Self-Guided Contract, they could mark these forms in the appropriate squares to become aware of many things they ought to work on during the next quarter. They could also be used during departmental meetings to help develop the agenda. The questions on these forms are simply a beginning; you may add your own statements concerning sound Christian education, then phrase a question that causes teachers to see if they are practicing those principles.

Teacher: ask someone to sit in your class session and objectively write down what he sees happen. The observer shouldn't make any value judgments, but record only the facts. When you have the facts before you, *you* can make the value judgments about the effectiveness of your teaching. Remember, you never see yourself in action as you really are. Provide this observation/evaluation sheet as a guide for your friends' (and maybe even your departmental superintendent's) observation.

SELF-STUDY GUIDE

FOR PRESCHOOL DEPARTMENTS

☐ IMPROVEMENT NEEDED
☐ STARTED
☐ PROGRESS

I. TEACHER'S ROLE

☐ I ☐ S ☐ P   A. Realizing that Bible knowledge is scant, do you use objects constantly? Your pupils have a need to explore, touch, taste, look, smell and handle.

☐ I ☐ S ☐ P   B. Are Bible stories carefully differentiated from fanciful stories? (This is important since children do not easily distinguish between fact and fancy).

☐ I ☐ S ☐ P   C. The child needs security in one person. What are you doing to see that he has that security?

☐ I ☐ S ☐ P   D. Since children also find security in knowing what is *expected* of them, knowing what they can and cannot do, have you established limits for the use of materials? E.g., blocks remain in the block corner.

☐ I ☐ S ☐ P   E. Every child needs to be assured of your love and acceptance. Do you *listen* to him with your *eye-contact*?

☐ I ☐ S ☐ P   F. What have you done to get acquainted with the *mothers* and their children? For instance, a mother's tea or an open house. Do you make calls on all of your students, even those who are not absentees?

63

☐ I ☐ S ☐ P **G.** Since *men* are given the custodial task as moral and spiritual leaders, do you have men in your department working with the children? Remember, a child's life-style is, to a large degree, set by the time he is six. A man's presence gives strong non-verbal communication about the church being also for men.

☐ I ☐ S ☐ P **H.** Closely associated with a child's "energy need" is his need for *sensory stimulation.* Are you regularly allowing him to be exposed to many forms and media?

☐ I ☐ S ☐ P **I.** For young children to feel a relationship with God, they need to experience *forgiveness.* This is better done by experiencing the love and forgiveness of others. Are you teaching this in your department?

☐ I ☐ S ☐ P **J.** Those who guide young children must themselves be *teachable,* willing to learn. Do you keep abreast of today's educational trends by reading current articles, attending workshops geared to the children you teach?

II. SCHEDULE

☐ I ☐ S ☐ P **A.** Do you *change pace* enough so a child's interest is kept?

☐ I ☐ S ☐ P **B.** Since *play* has a definite purpose for the child, is your play period organized in such a way that your children are actually *learning* good things?

☐ I ☐ S ☐ P **C.** Does your *schedule* allow for the following:
—Alternating periods of rest and activity
—Flexibility within the structure of any day's schedule

—Opportunity for solitude

—A chance to cherish the old indefinitely and to move slowly into the new

—Physical safety and hygiene

—Time for person-to-person living, as well as teacher-group living

—Serenity and peacefulness in atmosphere

—Prayer, praise, and giving

—Do they see you act out the story in a way that properly projects the ideas to them?

☐ I ☐ S ☐ P D. What have you done to provide a presession for your children on their arrival at Bible school?

III. CHILD'S DEVELOPMENT

☐ I ☐ S ☐ P A. Do you allow a child to do the maximum amount for himself? He has one intuitive aim, his *self-development.* If a child is not allowed to follow his natural curiosity and his need to know, he loses interest.

☐ I ☐ S ☐ P B. Nursery children can learn *concepts* about God, Jesus, the Bible, themselves and their church. Are you doing all you can to help them relate these concepts to their own minds?

☐ I ☐ S ☐ P C. How much room do you give for an *individual* to be himself?

☐ I ☐ S ☐ P D. Having recognized that the operation of a department is a *team effort,* are you providing communication sessions like departmental staff meetings where the staff can pray and work to maintain total team input for planning and organization?

☐ I ☐ S ☐ P E. Since *parents* have the primary responsibility for their children's total education, have you discussed with them how you might join hands in their children's Christian education (including use of take-home papers and/or books)?

☐ I ☐ S ☐ P F. Is your reinforcement of behavior done in a positive way . . . "we keep the books in the reading area" rather than "don't take the books over there."

IV. FACILITY

☐ I ☐ S ☐ P A. Does your room create an *atmosphere* of love, security and joy which associates genuine gladness with God's house?

☐ I ☐ S ☐ P B. Have you cared for all the necessary sanitation problems? Are the toys cleaned regularly? bedding changed? floor scrubbed?

☐ I ☐ S ☐ P C. There has never been, in the history of man, an adult scientist half so *curious* as any child between the ages of 18 months and four years. Half the intellectual capacity of an adult has been developed by the age of four. Do you give them plenty of opportunity to gain that kind of learning experience in such things as an interest center?

"I took a piece of plastic clay
And idly fashioned it one day.
And as my fingers pressed it still,
It bent and yielded to my will.
I came again when days had passed,
That lump of clay was hard at last,
The form I gave it, still it bore,
But I could change it nevermore.

I took a child, God's living clay,
And gently shaped it day by day
And moulded with my Saviour's art
A young child's soft and yielding heart.
I came again when years were gone.
He was a man I looked upon.
But still that early image bore,
But I could change him nevermore."
                    —Author unknown

SELF-STUDY GUIDE

FOR GRADE SCHOOL DEPARTMENTS

☐ IMPROVEMENT NEEDED

☐ STARTED

☐ PROGRESS

I. PRESESSION

☐ I ☐ S ☐ P **A.** Recognizing that children do not primarily need a social hour, do you engage them in meaningful *learning activity* as soon as they arrive in the building?

☐ I ☐ S ☐ P **B.** Since *variety* helps to stimulate the mind and to motivate attendance, how is the teaching session given to variety?

1. Murals on the quarterly theme.
2. Memory contest
3. Building a Bible city
4. Exciting continued story
5. Missionary interest-corner
6. Printing picture with verse for the day
7. Developing a "Hall of Answered Prayer"
8. Show slides or short movies
9. Making scrolls
10. Browsing in books
11. Bible puzzles—both making and assembling

☐ I ☐ S ☐ P **C.** Knowing that additional time with the students is valuable, are all teachers present to *meet the students* as they arrive?

II. ASSEMBLY

☐ I ☐ S ☐ P **A.** The assembly is an activity for the entire department. Are the teachers taking part in the *planning* and worship experience?

☐ I ☐ S ☐ P **B.** The assembly period is not to be used by the superintendent to teach a separate lesson. Are these sessions really *preparing* the students for the lesson time with their teachers?

☐ I ☐ S ☐ P **C.** Is the time so scheduled that the teachers have *adequate time* for the lessons?

☐ I ☐ S ☐ P **D.** In order that the children might sense that this is their school, are their talents used? Do they have opportunity to *participate?* Do you highlight them in the program from time to time?

☐ I ☐ S ☐ P **E.** Children need to become acquainted with a *variety of music.* Do you teach them "new" hymns as well as choruses? Do you visualize songs?

☐ I ☐ S ☐ P **F.** Knowing that many children do not experience a meaningful worship time, have you developed a *worship center?* Do you include worship experiences regularly? Are you building in them a sense of reverence for the house of God?

☐ I ☐ S ☐ P **G.** Routine can be a death-trap. Does your weekly plan include sufficient variety?

☐ I ☐ S ☐ P **H.** Since the facility sets the *atmosphere,* is your room neat, orderly, and properly decorated?

☐ I ☐ S ☐ P **I.** Children begin to formulate valuable impressions of the work of *missions.* Have you introduced them to the missionaries who are supported by your church and given them an intro-

☐ I ☐ S ☐ P

ductory understanding of missions?

J. Have you given them an opportunity to become personally *involved in missions?* (Giving, projects, missionary scrapbook, sharing Christ with others, etc.)

III. TEACHING STUDENTS

☐ I ☐ S ☐ P

A. Does the aim or life-response goal so permeate each lesson that each student goes home knowing exactly what God *expects* of him as a result of this Bible lesson?

☐ I ☐ S ☐ P

B. Is your *contact* with each student during the week geared to augment the life response goal?

☐ I ☐ S ☐ P

C. Do you *change* activity often enough during each session to maintain interest and prevent restlessness?

☐ I ☐ S ☐ P

D. Recognizing that the room decor aids or hinders the communication process, do you change the decorations in your classroom often, and is it kept orderly and attractive?

☐ I ☐ S ☐ P

E. Recognizing that your students live in a world penetrated by visual communication, do you constantly use meaningful *visuals?* Remember that greater learning is facilitated by appealing to more senses.

☐ I ☐ S ☐ P

F. Recognizing that you are what you read and that your lessons are, in a sense, a projection of your own life as well as the life of Christ, do you regularly *read* Christian periodicals? The list should include pedagogy, Christian enrichment periodicals, and books.

☐ I ☐ S ☐ P

G. Recognizing that your students must "take" any new truth they get and that you can't give them truth they won't "take," do you constantly engage them in *discovery projects* in the class? (Including role-playing, discussions, research, etc.)

☐ I ☐ S ☐ P H. Because you believe students must have a voice in the policies which regulate their lives, do you let them become involved in setting up *rules* for their classroom?

☐ I ☐ S ☐ P I. Because you understand that all students are not motivated to be interested in each lesson, do you become *acquainted* with each student so that you know the unique way he perceives things?

☐ I ☐ S ☐ P J. Realizing that your students need freedom and self-expression, do you give ample opportunity for each student to be engaged in *expression?*

☐ I ☐ S ☐ P K. Recognizing the part the Holy Spirit plays in a child's behavioral change, are you *praying* weekly for each child?

☐ I ☐ S ☐ P L. Since parents have the primary responsibility of their children's total education, have you discussed with them how you might join hands together in their children's Christian education (including take-home papers and/or books)?

☐ I ☐ S ☐ P M. Since learning will only proceed from the known to the unknown, what provisions have you made for a *new child* who has little or no Bible background?

IV. STAFF

☐ I ☐ S ☐ P A. A departmental operation should be a *team effort*. Do all on the staff have a part in the future plans of all departmental activities?

☐ I ☐ S ☐ P B. Do the teachers have opportunity to *share* their blessings and needs with all other staff members?

☐ I ☐ S ☐ P C. A superintendent cannot direct a department well unless he is aware of class activities. Does the superintendent *visit* each class at least once each quarter?

☐ I ☐ S ☐ P D. Have you enjoyed a special *outing* for your whole department during the last quarter? Did each class have an outing with its teacher?

SELF-STUDY GUIDE

FOR YOUTH DEPARTMENTS

☐ IMPROVEMENT NEEDED

☐ STARTED

☐ PROGRESS

I. ASSEMBLY

☐ I ☐ S ☐ P A. Youth must feel that the youth department is theirs. Are you giving them a *voice in the planning* and the the program presentation?

☐ I ☐ S ☐ P B. Music can greatly liven any youth gathering and can spiritually strengthen their lives. Does your weekly schedule provide for a *varied diet* of sound Christian music?

☐ I ☐ S ☐ P C. Assemblies should serve as *pacesetters* for the class session; does yours set the stage for a good teaching-learning situation?

☐ I ☐ S ☐ P D. Sunday school should be *fun*. It not only builds a good image but learning will more likely take place in a happy atmosphere. Is your department and class a fun place to be?

II. ORGANIZATION AND SCHEDULE

☐ I ☐ S ☐ P A. Each sex *relates* best to its own kind in the discipling process. Have you taken appropriate steps to see that each student relates to his own kind?

☐ I ☐ S ☐ P B. Youth need *fellowship* experiences continually. Are you facilitating that need?

☐ I ☐ S ☐ P   C. Youth are most often excited about events in which they have a part *in the planning.* Are you serving as a coach rather than a chief in the program and social affairs?

☐ I ☐ S ☐ P   D. Are your *records* complete and up to date so that you can keep track of each student?

III. TEACHING AND LEARNING

☐ I ☐ S ☐ P   A. The *setting* of the group either hinders or facilitates the learning process. Are you regularly giving concern about the chair arrangement to encourage group interaction?

☐ I ☐ S ☐ P   B. *Methods* are teaching tools. Are you continually adding new ones to your tool box? The lesson objectives should help guide your choices.

☐ I ☐ S ☐ P   C. The units of study in each quarter include a designed *behavioral change.* Are you personally interacting with the students under your charge to help them develop those spiritual behavioral patterns?

☐ I ☐ S ☐ P   D. Since the students remember what they see far more than what they only hear, are you constantly using projected and non-projected *visuals?*

☐ I ☐ S ☐ P   E. Most often truth does not become yours until it can be personally *verbalized.* Are you encouraging and providing students with the opportunity to do so?

☐ I ☐ S ☐ P   F. Since the very *environment of the room* will either hinder or facilitate a student's learning, have you brightened up your rooms so they say, "this is an enjoyable place to be"?

☐ I ☐ S ☐ P   G. When personally *motivated,* students

will become involved in personal research projects to aid in upcoming lessons and will carry on their own Bible studies. Are you providing the motivation and opportunities?

☐ I ☐ S ☐ P H. When students *discover Bible truth* on their own, it will be far more meaningful for them. Are you serving as a catalyst in that process?

☐ I ☐ S ☐ P I. When a *new student* attends, he will find it hard to comprehend advanced biblical thought without adequate background. Have you made arrangements to meet him at his learning level?

IV. RELATIONSHIPS

☐ I ☐ S ☐ P A. A good teacher strives together with the Holy Spirit in the discipling process. Are you *praying* faithfully for each student? (Col. 1:29)

☐ I ☐ S ☐ P B. Christian *values* are built into the lives of students through strong interpersonal relationships. Is each student being related to by a warm, strong Christian adult?

☐ I ☐ S ☐ P C. Is each student made to *feel a part* of the group or is he embarrassed or put on the spot?

☐ I ☐ S ☐ P D. Since *parents* have the primary responsibility of their children's total education, have you discussed with them either as a group or individually how you might join hands and hearts in their youths' education?

V. STAFF

☐ I ☐ S ☐ P A. A strong youth department is a *team* of caring adults who learn and work together. Are ample opportunities provided for your team to pray, study, and plan together?

☐ I ☐ S ☐ P B. A teacher never truly sees all the strengths and weaknesses of his teaching. Have you asked for an honest evaluation from other competent leaders and students?

SELF-STUDY GUIDE

FOR THE ADULT DEPARTMENT

☐ IMPROVEMENT NEEDED
☐ STARTED
☐ PROGRESS

I. PREPARATIONS

☐ I ☐ S ☐ P   A. All staff should constantly be upgrading their *teaching ability*. Are you providing for that to occur each year by offering courses of training?

☐ I ☐ S ☐ P   B. Recognizing that teachers must have a solid grasp of the Scripture they are going to teach, are you studying many *sources* to become an authority on each text and lesson taught?

II. ORGANIZATION

☐ I ☐ S ☐ P   A. Each class should have a *balanced diet* of Old and New Testament, Bible related subjects, Doctrine and Christian life. Have you given care to see that each adult has had that balance?

☐ I ☐ S ☐ P   B. When a *newcomer* steps into a new classroom situation, are you easing his insecurity by taking steps to make him immediately feel a part of the class (not putting him on the spot or embarrassing him)?

☐ I ☐ S ☐ P   C. Seating arrangements facilitate or hinder group interaction in the classroom, so do you move the chairs to break up a lecture setting?

☐ I ☐ S ☐ P   D. The Adult Department should be a

team effort. Are you providing communication sessions where adult staff people can build and work to maintain total team for planning and organization?

☐ I ☐ S ☐ P E. Since adults have reached different levels of spiritual maturity and have had various levels of exposure to Bible knowledge, are you offering *different levels of training* in the Adult Department to meet those needs?

☐ I ☐ S ☐ P F. Adults learn when they sense a study is meeting their *life's needs.* Have you asked recently for a written tabulation of their feelings about that?

III. CLASS SESSION

☐ I ☐ S ☐ P A. An Adult Bible school should be a missionary training and sending station. Are you helping your disciples to actually become *involved missionaries?* (Matthew 28:19-20)

☐ I ☐ S ☐ P B. I am constantly practicing the concept that I will not do anything for the student that he can *do for himself.*

☐ I ☐ S ☐ P C. To study the Bible without the objective of developing personal spiritual *maturity* and/or ministering to others could end up only as an exercise in stockpiling religious information. Is all your instruction really that practical? (2 Timothy 2:14-16)

☐ I ☐ S ☐ P D. The sooner we can put into *practice* what we have learned, the more apt we are to learn those truths. Have you provided practical guidelines for the implementation of each learning section? (A section includes knowing, feeling, and doing in a group of one or more lessons.)

☐ I ☐ S ☐ P
E. Because faith comes by "hearing the Word of God," have you made each lesson an experience in hearing a *word from God?* (Romans 10:17)

☐ I ☐ S ☐ P
F. Because adults resist being told what to do, have you constantly structured your teaching conclusion in such a way that your students will definitely make their *own application* and follow through with it?

☐ I ☐ S ☐ P
G. Recognizing that expression helps a student to internalize the truth, has each one of your adults actually *expressed* himself either verbally or in writing on a regular basis? (Joshua 1:8)

☐ I ☐ S ☐ P
H. Because *variety of experience* in learning is a key factor in motivating a learner, have you used a constant variety of teaching methods? Have you provided a variety of student-learning experiences?

☐ I ☐ S ☐ P
I. Today, more than ever before, adults are accustomed to receiving their communication via *multimedia.* Are you constantly using a variety of these innumerable multimedia in your lesson presentations?

☐ I ☐ S ☐ P
J. Since adults are highly *creative,* are you constantly providing that kind of opportunity in your class?

IV. RELATIONSHIPS

☐ I ☐ S ☐ P
A. Because each decade of adults have different *tension points* and *social needs,* are you seeking to provide them the kind of program and teaching that meets those needs?

☐ I ☐ S ☐ P
B. Each adult comes with a need for *intimacy.* Are you providing some

sort of care group where they find personal warmth and face-to-face confrontation? Do you show them somehow that somebody really cares for them? (What about when they are absent, ill, or have a personal family need?)

☐ I ☐ S ☐ P   C. Recognizing the work of the Holy Spirit in developing behavioral change, are you *praying* regularly for the spiritual development of each class member?

☐ I ☐ S ☐ P   D. Knowing that you can only adequately lead the teaching/learning situations in your class as you know the *perceptual mechanism* of each student, are you becoming better acquainted with your students outside the classroom?

☐ I ☐ S ☐ P   E. Recognizing that students seldom follow through with implementing the application, are you augmenting your lesson's *life-goals* by relating to the class members during the week?

Class_____

OBSERVATION-EVALUATION SHEET

1. Use of materials in teaching:	7. Relationship of biblical subject matter to life situations:
2. Opportunity for student participation:	8. Student inquiry into subject matter:
3. Attitude toward opinion of students:	9. Recognition of learning difficulties:
4. Developing physical environment:	10. Rapport with students:
5. Teacher preparation for class session:	11. Developing student skills in Bible use and Bible helps:
6. Variety in learning activities:	12. Classroom control:

POST CONFERENCE QUESTIONS:

Observer:_____

EVALUATION OF THE
TEACHING/LEARNING PROCESS

Realizing that this evaluation will be subjective, nevertheless it will serve as a useful tool in trying to better understand the teaching/learning process. If you feel that you are not qualified to make a judgment on an item, you may omit it.

1. A general air of FRIENDLINESS and happiness pervades the classroom.

Friendliness___:___:___:___:___:___ Lack of friendliness

2. Enthusiasm stimulates class interest.

Enthusiasm___:___:___:___:___:___ Lack of enthusiasm

3. The teacher uses personal examples, and is willing to admit personal shortcomings.

Honest___:___:___:___:___:___Lack of honesty

4. HUMOR in the classroom tends to promote more effective learning.

Humor___:___:___:___:___:___Lack of humor

5. Clear and commanding SPEAKING by everyone aids our learning.

Good speech___:___:___:___:___:___ Poor speech

6. FREEDOM FROM ANNOYANCES in the classroom contributes to the effectiveness of the teaching/learning situation.

Freedom from
annoyances ___:___:___:___:___ Bothered by annoyances

7. The PROMPTNESS and efficiency of the instructor increases the value of the class.

Promptness___:___:___:___:___:___Lack of promptness

8. The general APPEARANCE and demeanor of the teacher are appropriate.

Good appearance___:___:___:___:___:___Poor appearance

9. The working relationships of the staff are complementary to each other, and add to the UNITY of the teaching/learning process.

Unity___:___:___:___:___:___Disunity

10. The teacher maintains good learning discipline in his classroom.

Good discipline___:___:___:___:___:___Poor discipline

11. The purpose of the course is clear to the students.

Clear purpose___:___:___:___:___:___Unclear purpose

12. The instructor's preparation appears adequate.

Good preparation___:___:___:___:___:___Poor preparation

13. Classroom activities are orderly and systematic.

Good organization___:___:___:___:___:___Poor organization

14. Assignments are clear and challenging.

Good assignments___:___:___:___:___:___Poor assignments

15. Teaching methods are appropriate.

Appropriate___:___:___:___:___:___Not appropriate

List methods used: _____

_____

_____

_____

_____

16. Students participate actively in class procedures.

Participate___:___:___:___:___:___Do not participate

17. The class is related to daily life.

Applicable___:___:___:___:___:___Not applicable

18. Outlines, syllabi, summaries, and other supplementary materials contribute to student learning.

Aids, materials___:___:___:___:___:___Lack of aids and
                                                          materials

19. Sufficient time is provided for REVIEW.

Review time___:___:___:___:___:___No review time

20. Does the teacher really LISTEN to his students?

Listens___:___:___:___:___:___Does not really listen

21. The objectives of the teacher were reached.

Objectives reached___:___:___:___:___:___Objectives not
                                                                  reached

(Ask ahead of time and see if you think he reached them during the class.)

22. The spiritual tone of the class:

Highly spiritual___:___:___:___:___:___Purely secular

23. The authority in the classroom was:

Word of God___:___:___:___:___:___Teacher

Name of Evaluator:_____Date:_____

SUNDAY SCHOOL EVALUATION SHEET

Pastor and General Superintendent

A. ADMINISTRATION

1. Number of years served as superintendent:_____

2. Have you had an organized visitation program in your Sunday School within the last year?_____For how long?_____Comments on the success or failure of the program:_____

_____

_____

3. List areas where you feel Sunday School needs the greatest help:_____

_____

_____

4. In what way do you work in cooperation with the pastor in the planning and operation of the Sunday School?

_____

_____

_____

5. What have you been doing to evaluate the effectiveness of your school?_____

_____

_____

B. STAFF

1. List additional general staff members:

	Term of Office	How Chosen

2. How are the teachers selected for your Sunday School?

_____

_____

_____

_____

3. Are all of your teachers, NOT UNDER TEMPORARY APPOINTMENTS, members of your church?_____

4. How often do you have a Sunday School staff meeting?

_____

What percent of your staff attend?_____

List the normal agenda of your meetings:_____

_____

_____

5. What type of teacher substitute program do you have?

_____

6. Does your Sunday School have a Teacher's Standard or covenant?_____

What is being done to enforce these standards?_____

_____

_____

C. CURRICULUM

1. What material are you now using? (If more than one material, list them by department.)_____

_____

_____

2. Who makes the choice on this material?＿＿＿＿＿＿

3. Has your Sunday School sponsored or participated in at least one systematic training course during the past year?＿＿＿＿＿＿＿＿＿＿＿＿＿＿＿＿＿＿＿＿＿＿

Courses Taught	Teacher	Enrollment

4. What is being done in your Sunday School to promote a missionary education program?＿＿＿＿＿＿＿＿＿＿＿

＿＿＿＿＿＿＿＿＿＿＿＿＿＿＿＿＿＿＿＿＿＿＿＿＿＿

5. Have you used any form of the elective system in your adult or youth department? Comment on its effectiveness:

＿＿＿＿＿＿＿＿＿＿＿＿＿＿＿＿＿＿＿＿＿＿＿＿＿＿

＿＿＿＿＿＿＿＿＿＿＿＿＿＿＿＿＿＿＿＿＿＿＿＿＿＿

D. ORGANIZATION

1. List the departments that meet separately in your Sunday School:＿＿＿＿＿＿＿＿＿＿＿＿＿＿＿＿＿

_____

_____

2. a. Do you have one teacher for every 5 to 8 pupils in your Nursery and Pre-primary (4s and 5s) Departments?_____

   b. Do you have one teacher for every 8 pupils in your Primary and Junior Departments?_____

   c. Do you have at least one teacher for every 10 to 12 pupils in your Junior High and High School Departments?

3. List the beginning and closing hours of your Sunday School:_____

4. What special days do you observe as a Sunday School by having special all-school programs?_____

_____

_____

E. FACILITIES

1. Do you have a Church or Sunday School library that contains leadership training books? Are they actively circulating among your teachers and officers?_____

_____

2. Does your church have a visual aid library for your Sunday School workers?_____

3. What additional departmental and class room spaces are needed? _____

_____

F. PUPILS

How many of your Sunday School pupils became members of your church during the past year?_____

2. Do at least 70% of your pupils above 8 years of age attend the worship services (either church or children's church)? _____

What provision is made for worship for your children during the church hour?_____

_____

G. RECORDS

1. List the kinds of records you keep of your Sunday School. (Attach copies of all forms you use.)

_____

_____

_____

2. Do you keep a permanent master record of each pupil in the Sunday School?_____

H. FINANCES

1. How Sunday School expenses are paid:

___a. Church general account

___b. A separate Sunday School account

___c. Other _____

2. Sunday School offerings are placed in:

___a. The church general account

___b. A separate Sunday School account

___c. The mission fund

___d. Other _____

3. The school's budget is developed:

___a. As part of the church budget

___b. Separate from the church budget

ESTABLISHING A STANDARD FOR
THE SUNDAY SCHOOL

When an evaluation is conducted, it immediately suggests a standard. The Word of God gives us an overall standard for teaching the Word of God itself, both what we teach and some guidelines about how it ought to be taught. Beyond that, a school should establish its own guidelines for uniformity of operation and top efficiency. The following questions will help establish a guideline to check the efficiency of your school. As you answer these questions, do so in the light of the kind of teacher God would have you to be. Please indicate the following:

_____Teacher_____Superintendent_____Other: _____

A. A SUNDAY SCHOOL WORKER'S LIFE

1. A teacher should spend how many hours in preparation each week? (Circle the amount.)

   1   2   3   4   5   6   7   8   9   10   more

2. Each worker should be on the job on Sunday by:

   __half an hour before starting time

   __15 minutes before starting time

   __at starting time

   other _____

3. Each worker should be faithful in attendance at the Sunday:

   __a.m. Worship Service

——p.m. Worship Service

——Midweek Service

4. Each worker should faithfully spend time in prayer and Bible study as follows:

——once or more daily

——once weekly

——less than once weekly

B. STUDENT CONTACTS

1. A teacher should maintain contact with *absent* students outside the class:

    a. ——by phone

    b. ——by home visits

    c. ——by mail

    d. ——by parties, etc.

    e. ——make none

    f. ——other _____

2. A teacher should maintain contact with the *faithful* attenders outside the class:

——once a week

——once a month

——yearly

——not necessary

3. A teacher should maintain contact with the faithful attenders outside the class:

   a. __by phone

   b. __by home visits

   c. __by mail

   d. __by parties, etc.

   e. __make none

   f. __feel it is unnecessary

4. Generally my private discussions with my students after class or during the week deal with:

   a. __factual content of the Bible lesson taught currently

   b. __items of miscellaneous interest only

   c. __their attendance at church or Sunday School

   d. __their class behavior

   e. __the practical application of the current lesson to aid their relationship to and growth in Christ

C. TEACHING AIDS

1. While teaching, a teacher should regularly use:

   __non-projected visuals (charts, flannelgraph, chalkboards, maps, pictures)

   __projected visuals (movies, filmstrips, overhead projector)

   __not needed

2. While preparing to teach the lesson, a teacher should (check one or more):

___study the Bible and quarterly

___use additional references

___select a lesson of your own choosing

___consistently teach the assigned curriculum

3. How many hours of teacher training should a teacher take each year? (Circle your answer.)

0 1 2 3 4 5 6 7 8 9 10 11 12 13 14 15 more

4. A staff meeting should be held:
   a. For our department:

   ___monthly   ___bimonthly   ___unnecessary

   ___quarterly   ___annually

   b. For the whole staff:

   ___monthly   ___bimonthly   ___unnecessary

   ___quarterly   ___annually

D. ACCOUNTABILITY

In order for a Bible school to operate effectively in matters of teaching, contacts, curriculum, attendance, etc., a teacher should be guided by and held accountable (check one):

To God through
___a Bible school standard
and covenant

To God through
___a pastor

To God through
___a superintendent

___ none other than God

E. STANDARD

A teacher's concern about the conversion of his students will be shown by (mark only one of two):

    a. ___talking privately with each student about receiving Christ

    b. ___waiting for the student to take the initiative in receiving Christ

(mark only one of two)

    a. ___regularly giving a public invitation to receive Christ

    b. ___giving a public invitation to receive Christ when the lesson objective stresses it

TEACHER EVALUATION

(Circle the right
answer or fill in
the blank)

A. MY CLASS

1. Age or grade of class   1. _____

2. Sex (M-Male F-Female   2. _____
   C-Coed)

3. How many years have you   3. _____
   taught in Sunday School?

4. How many years have you   4. _____
   taught *this* class?

5. Do you like teaching this class?   5.   Yes   No

6. If "no" on 5, what age would   6. _____
   you prefer?

B. CLASSROOM FACILITY

1. My classroom space is adequate.   1.   Yes   No

2. The room's furniture is   2.   Yes   No
   adequate.

3. I have a chalkboard in my   3.   Yes   No
   room.

4. I need the following additional   4. _____
   equipment: _____

                              _____

5. I periodically change decora-   5.   Yes   No
   tions and room arrangement.

C. TEACHER'S TIME

1. My average preparation time is: 1. _____

2. I feel my preparation time is adequate. 2. Yes No

3. I would spend more time in preparation but: 3. _____

    a. I work long hours. a. _____

    b. I have other church responsibilities. b. _____

    c. I don't know what else to study. c. _____

    d. I don't have books necessary for study. d. _____

4. I am normally at Sunday School 15 minutes before it starts. 4. Yes No

5. I would come earlier but: 5. _____

    a. My family hinders me. a. _____

    b. I pick up riders. b. _____

    c. I don't think it's important. c. _____

    d. I don't plan my time right. d. _____

    e. Other reason. e. _____

6. The amount of teaching time is: 6. _____

    a. Adequate a. _____

    b. Inadequate b. _____

7. I habitually attend the follow-   7. _____
ing church services:

   a. a.m.   a. _____

   b. p.m.   b. _____

   c. Midweek   c. _____

8. I habitually spend time person-   8. _____
ally in prayer and Bible reading:

   a. Once each day or more   a. _____

   b. Once weekly   b. _____

   c. Less than once weekly   c. _____

D. STUDENT CONTACTS

1. How I keep in contact with   1. _____
my absentees:

   a. By phone   a. _____

   b. By home visits   b. _____

   c. By mail   c. _____

   d. By outside contacts   d. _____

   e. Make none   e. _____

2. I do not contact my students   2. _____
outside the class because:

   a. I have no transportation.   a. _____

   b. I'm afraid to visit.   b. _____

c. I don't think it's important.   c. _____

d. I don't have time.   d. _____

e. Someone else does it for me.   e. _____

3. How I contact my regular   3. _____
   students:

   a. By phone   a. _____

   b. By home visits   b. _____

   c. By mail   c. _____

   d. By outside contacts   d. _____

   e. Make none   e. _____

4. Generally my private discus-   4. _____
   sions with my students after
   class or during the week deal
   with:

   a. Factual content of Bible   a. _____
      lesson taught currently

   b. Items of miscellaneous   b. _____
      interest only

   c. Their attendance at church   c. _____
      or Sunday School

   d. Their class behavior   d. _____

   e. The practical application   e. _____
      of the current lesson to
      aid their relationship to
      and growth in Christ

E. TEACHING METHODS

1. I have used the following at least once during the past three months: 1. _____

    a. Lecture a. _____

    b. Discussion b. _____

    c. Projected (slides, movies, overhead transparencies) c. _____

    d. Non-projected (charts, flannelgraph, chalkboard, maps) d. _____

    e. Creative writing e. _____

    f. Panel discussion, debate, forum f. _____

    g. Inductive Bible study g. _____

    h. Instructive play h. _____

    i. Field trip i. _____

    j. Storytelling j. _____

    k. Object lesson k. _____

    l. Buzz groups l. _____

    m. Role play (student) m. _____

    n. Research or projects n. _____

    o. Question and answer o. _____

    p. Written quiz p. _____

2. I do not use any visuals be- 2. _____
cause: (only if applicable)

   a. The church does not provide a. _____
them.

   b. I do not have the time to b. _____
get them ready.

   c. I feel they are unnecessary. c. _____

3. When I present my lesson, I 3. _____
usually:

   a. Teach from my notes. a. _____

   b. Teach from the Bible only. b. _____

   c. Teach from quarterly and c. _____
Bible only.

   d. Read the lesson to students. d. _____

4. I frequently use reference 4.   Yes   No
books in lesson preparation.

5. I don't use any references 5. _____
because:

   a. I don't have any. a. _____

   b. I don't see the need for b. _____
them.

   c. The church doesn't have c. _____
any.

   d. Other _____ d. _____

6. The theme of the departmental 6.   Yes   No

assembly is correlated with my
lesson.

F. STUDENTS IN SESSION

1. I try to actively involve my students in each class session.

    1.   Yes   No

2. I have given my students a specific assignment to put into practice a life-related learning activity at least once during the past 6 weeks.

    2.   Yes   No

3. My students are given work-books.

    3.   Yes   No

4. I do not give them workbooks to use at home because:

    4. _____

    a. We work on them in class.

        a. _____

    b. They won't use them.

        b. _____

    c. I don't like them.

        c. _____

    d. They are not provided by the church.

        d. _____

    e. Other reasons _____

        e. _____

G. STAFF TRAINING

1. My training in teaching techniques includes:

    1. _____

    a. One course

        a. _____

    b. Two or more courses

        b. _____

   c. Extensive training   c. _____

   d. No courses   d. _____

2. I sense that I need more   2. _____
   training in:

   a. Teaching techniques   a. _____

   b. Bible background   b. _____

3. My greatest need in teaching   3. _____

   at this time is: _____

4. I usually attend the general   4.   Yes   No
   staff meetings.

5. I usually attend the depart-   5.   Yes   No
   mental staff meetings.

6. I don't attend staff meetings   6. _____
   because:

   a. They don't meet my needs.   a. _____

   b. I have a conflict of schedule.   b. _____

   c. I have no transportation.   c. _____

   d. We don't have them.   d. _____

H. STUDENT EVANGELISM

1. The number of students in my 1. _____
   class who have made a personal
   commitment to Christ this year
   is:

2. To my knowledge all my stu-   2.   Yes   No

dents have accepted Christ as
their Saviour.

3. a. I have privately talked with   3. a. _____
each student about salva-
tion.

b. I have given an appeal in   b. _____
class.

c. I don't know how to lead a   c. _____
pupil to Christ.

d. My students are too young.   d. _____

I. STUDENT GROWTH
My students' spiritual growth
could be characterized as:

a. Reading Bible more   a. _____

b. Praying more   b. _____

c. Attitude changes   c. _____

d. More dedicated to Christ   d. _____

e. More spiritual interest   e. _____

f. Witnessing more   f. _____

g. Less interested   g. _____

h. No way to observe them   h. _____

J. STUDENT DISCIPLINE
1. During class my students usually   1. _____
are:

a. Quiet   a. _____

b. Hard to control   b. _____

c. Quiet, but do not participate   c. _____

d. Cooperative and participa-   d. _____

   tive

2. I sometimes have difficulty   2. _____
   keeping order because:

   a. The students are not   a. _____
      interested in the lesson.

   b. I don't know how to keep   b. _____
      order.

   c. Other classes are distracting. c. _____

   d. Students are unruly.   d. _____

WHAT'S HAPPENING TO ME?

(Student Questionnaire)

Teacher's Name_____ Grade_____

Class: Male_____ Female_____ Coed_____

Have you committed your life to Christ? Yes_____ No_____

The value of this Sunday School is best tested by what is happening in your spiritual life. By answering the following questions you will help us to determine that value. Please circle the number along the top line that best describes what is happening to you as a result of your involvement in Sunday School. Since your name will not be asked, you can be assured that this information will not be identified with you. (No. 1 is the strongest or best and No. 6 is the weakest or poorest.)

1. I feel that I have a strong personal relationship with my teacher.

   strong relationship 1 2 3 4 5 6 *weak relationship*

2. My teacher has an active interest in the progress of the development of my spiritual life.

   active interest 1 2 3 4 5 6 *less active interest*

3. I feel free to discuss my doubts and questions regarding Christianity with my teacher.

   to a higher degree 1 2 3 4 5 6 *to a lesser degree*

4. The weekly lessons are valuable to me.

   valuable 1 2 3 4 5 6 *not valuable*

5. I freely participate in the class discussions.

   weekly 1 2 3 4 5 6 *never*

6. I apply the Bible lesson to my life.

   every lesson   1   2   3   4   5   6   *never*

7. My Sunday School experience "feeds me" spiritually and provides for growth in my Christian life.

   weekly   1   2   3   4   5   6   *never*

8. I come to class because:

   __I am forced to come.

   __I enjoy Bible study.

   __I want to see friends.

   __Of habit.

   __Other reason: _____

9. I would be a better student if:

   _____

   _____

   _____

10. My spiritual growth, as a direct result of involvement in this class, could be described as:

    __a. Becoming less interested

    __b. No interest

    __c. Reading my Bible more

    __d. Praying more

    __e. Changing attitudes

    __f. Dedication to Christ increased

___g. More spiritual interest

___h. Witnessing more

11. If you think of a *likeable* quality or habit possessed by your instructor please add it in the space below:

_____

_____

_____

_____

_____

DEPARTMENT SUPERINTENDENT QUESTIONNAIRE

A. ORGANIZATION

1. What grades or ages are included in your department?

   _____

2. How long have you been superintendent of *this department?* _____

3. How long have you been a Department Superintendent? _____How long have you taught in Sunday School? _____

4. List your class divisions:

Age or Grade	Class Name	Boys, Girls, Coed	Average Attendance

5. List additional personnel in department other than teach-

    ers: _____

6. Does your department have its own assembly?_____

    If not, what other groups do you meet with?_____

    _____

7. Do you have departmental staff meetings in addition to

    the entire Sunday School staff meetings?_____

8. List a simple agenda of your session with your staff:

    _____

    _____

    _____

9. Who keeps the records in your department?_____

    _____

    What records do you keep?_____

    What use do you make of the information you gather

    from the records?_____

    _____

10. Do you try to correlate the theme of your assembly with

    your teachers' lessons?_____

11. Describe any presession (prior to starting time) activity

you have: _____

Who takes this responsibility? _____

12. What is being done to encourage the parents' cooperation in helping the students study their lessons at home?

    _____

    _____

13. What added equipment or facilities do you need in your department? _____

    _____

B. TEACHERS

1. How often do you visit the classes in your department?

   __Never __Monthly __Quarterly __Annually __I teach, so can't.

2. Are your teachers following the prescribed curriculum?

   _____

3. What help do you feel your teachers need to help them in communicating their lessons? _____

   _____

4. How are teachers selected in your department? _____

   _____

5. What part do your teachers play in the departmental as-

sembly each Sunday? _____

_____

6. What kind of teacher substitute program do you have?

_____

7. What have you been doing to help your teachers to improve? _____

C. PROGRAM

1. How much time do you usually have for the departmental assembly? _____

2. What curriculum guides are used for the assembly?

_____

3. What do you consider to be the purpose of the departmental assembly? _____

_____

_____

4. What help do you need in better carrying out the purpose of the assembly? _____

_____

_____

5. Have you had any departmental contest during the last

12 months? _____

What kind? _____

With what results? _____

6. Do you have a Scripture memorization plan for the department? _____

   If so, give details: _____

   _____

7. What do you do as a department in the way of Missionary Education? _____

   _____

   _____

8. Our assembly begins: __Rarely on time __Usually on time __Always on time

D. PUPILS

1. How do your pupils take part in the assembly, other than in singing and reading parts? _____

   _____

2. What extra departmental activities do you have for the pupils during the year? _____

   _____

3. What do you do to make visitors feel welcome? _____

_____

_____

RECORD OF ATTENDANCE

CHURCH:

CITY:

TOTAL SUNDAY SCHOOL
MONTHLY AVERAGE ATTENDANCE

YEAR	J A N	F E B	M A R	A P R	M A Y	J U N	J U L	A U G	S E P	O C T	N O V	D E C

SUNDAY SCHOOL ANNUAL AVERAGE ATTENDANCE

CHURCH A.M. ANNUAL AVERAGE ATTENDANCE

DEPARTMENTAL ANNUAL AVERAGE ATTENDANCE

Designate the names of the Sunday school departments according to your organization.

Gather as many statistics as possible. Try to complete the form for at least the last five years. Each additional piece of information will be that much more helpful in projecting strategy and goals.

CITY OR COMMUNITY PROFILE

Assemble as many of the following facts as you can about the area that you consider to be your responsibility of outreach. You may want to check with the City Hall, School District, or Chamber of Commerce for this profile information.

AGE GROUP	PRESCHOOL	GRADE SCHOOL	JUNIOR HIGH	HIGH SCHOOL	ADULTS TO 65	ADULTS 65 AND OVER	TOTAL POPULATION
PRESENT CENSUS 19___							

Train for Teaching and Administration with Victor Books How-To's

DATE DUE

JAN 6 '78			
FEB 20 '79			
DEC 18 '80			
MAR 2 1 '83			
MAR 2 6 '84			
APR 9 '84			
DEC 17 '84			
MAR 14 '85			
JUN 19 '87			
OCT 20 '88			
NOV 22 '88			
DEC 23 '88			
MY 6 '92			
JY 31 '97			

DEMCO 38-297